Unbound

A Devotional Anthology for Artemis

Compiled by Thista Minai
and the Editorial Board of
the Library of Neos Alexandria

Copyright © 2009 by Neos Alexandria

All rights reserved. No part of this book may be reproduced by any means or in any form whatsoever without written permission from the author(s), except for brief quotations embodied in literary articles or reviews. Copyright reverts to individual authors after publication.

To Artemis:

May many minds perceive what one cannot conceive.

Table of Contents

Introduction by Thista Minai 5

Hymn to Artemis Alexandria by Scott B. Wilson 7
Artemis by Amanda Sioux Blake 10
Artemis by Kenn Payne 20
The Virgin Goddess by Thista Minai 21
The Fertile Goddess by Thista Minai 26
Artemis Speaks by Melia Suez 31
Artemis of the Ephesians by Corbin 32
Invocations of Artemis by Rebecca Buchanan 34
My Life with Artemis by Lupa 36
Artemis and the Modern Man by Bronto Sproximo 41
Artemis by Thista Minai 45
A Tale of Two Gods by Frater Eleuthereus 47
Prayer for Artemis by Melia Suez 56
Hymn to Artemis of the Poisoned Earth by Rebecca
    Buchanan 57
Artemis Alpheia by Scott B. Wilson 58
Artemis and Lykastos by P. Sufenas Virius Lupus 61
Prayer to Artemis by Astalon 67
The Death of Actaeon by Jennifer Lawrence 69
Healing with Artemis by Amanda Sioux Blake 71
Touched by Artemis by Barbara Artemis Rachel 73
Choices by Allyson Szabo 76
Little Bears by Rebecca Buchanan 83
The Prayer of Kleia by Sannion 84
To Bless a Child by Frater Eleuthereus 86
Artemis, Destroyer by Allyson Szabo 88
Death and Dance by Thista Minai 89
Artemis & Orion by Kenn Payne 90
Hippolytus, Beloved of Artemis by Michael Routery 100
Artemis and the Cult of Antinous by P. Sufenas Virius
    Lupus 106

Finding a Shrine's Home by Allyson Szabo 113
To Artemis by Sannion 117
Analyzing the Role of Artemis the Huntress by Lykeia 118
Hunting the Snow by Paul Derrick 122
The Reflecting Pool by Michael Routery 124
My Experiences with Artemis by Melia Suez 129
Lady of the Cedar by Jennifer Lawrence 132
Artemis at Eleusis by Lykeia 133
Artemis and Dionysos: Antithesis and Synthesis by Thista Minai 135
Hymn to Artemis by Rev. Lady Bella Sundancer 140
Invocation to Artemis by E. A. Kaufman 141
Artemis by Corbin 142
Hymn to Artemis by Paul Derrick 143
Memoirs of a Huntress by Kayleigh Ayn Bohémier 144
Dianae Celticae by P. Sufenas Virius Lupus 147
Three Arrows by Jennifer Lawrence 151
Artemis Hêmerêsia by Frater Eleuthereus 159
Prayer and Devotion to Artemis by Bia' Aletheia 162
Artemis by Patrick Corrigan 164
Gavrel by Rebecca Buchanan 165
Artemis-Nemesis/Diana-Adrasteia by Frater Eleuthereus 175
The Savage Breast: Artemis of Ephesus by Tim Ward 177
Worshiper by Thista Minai 193

Suggested Reading 195
About the Bibliotheca Alexandrina 199

Introduction

by Thista Minai

On more than a few occasions people have come to me wanting to further develop their relationship with Artemis, and I was unable to help them. It wasn't that I had nothing to say, or that Artemis was not pertinent to them. My perspective in life was simply so different from theirs that my input could not be anything more than anecdotal. My relationship with Her was to them the sort of thing that's interesting to hear about but not something they would take part in themselves. It simply wasn't relevant. That is why I wanted to put together this book.

Artemis is such a magnificently immense Goddess that I think it's impossible for any one person to represent all of Her. No matter how hard I might try to show all Her aspects, illuminate all ways to approach Her, what I write will always be colored by my own mind, the way I perceive and conceive of myself, reality, and the Gods. In order to give people a truly multifaceted view of Artemis, I had to get input from other authors. I had to put together an anthology. Consequently this book is not mine; it belongs to everyone who contributed to it, and to Artemis Herself.

Because of the wonderful variety contained within this book, you'll find many differences in writing style, choice of spellings, theological perspective, and treatment of ancient material. I allowed submissions dedicated to Diana because although I personally see Her and Artemis as two separate deities, others disagree and consider them the same. Some people have written about Artemis in the ancient world and others have written about Artemis as she manifests in the modern world. I leave it up to the readers to determine which pieces of this anthology are pertinent to them. My only hope is that everyone can find at least one entry that is somehow helpful.

Finally, I would like to recognize the efforts of Sannion and Oinokhoe. Without their assistance in organization, editing, and design, this book would not exist. They both put in an incredible amount of time and energy behind the scenes, and deserve our gratitude.

I'll leave you with a zen story I've heard told and retold in many different ways:

Three blind men approach an elephant, having never seen one before. One man, feeling the trunk of the elephant, says "Elephants are long and flexible, like snakes." The next man, feeling the side of the elephant, says "Elephants are vast and flat, like walls." The third man, feeling a leg of the elephant, says "Elephants are round and sturdy, like trees."

I hope this book can help you see more of the elephant.

Hymn to Artemis Alexandria

by Scott B. Wilson

O Muse from Parnassian peak, inspire my words to the daughter
   of Zeus
Let me speak to the Lady with beauty and clarity and humility
Dearest Lady, these are the words I owe to You:

Artemis, far-shooting sister to the radiant God of my fathers,
You who were known to the Romans and Aricians as Diana,
brought to their rugged hills by Orestes from the Tauric shore,
although others sought You under eternal oaks long before
Many see You as huntress and virgin who dwells
far from mortal men where only beasts may survive,
but You are so much more and are known far and wide

Helper of Children, You kept my youthful innocence intact
and taught me about Nature's ways, neither cruel nor kind
Gentle and soothing, Leader of the Nymphs, Your trees
and creeks were my sanctuaries and sources of comfort
You guided me to save dogs and cats hungry and alone
You guided me to spare a baby bird from spinning wheels
You guided me to crush a suffering squirrel's skull

Goddess of the Lake, Goddess of the River
Goddess of the Marsh, Goddess of the Coast
Goddess of the Harbor, Goddess of Islands Remote

'Great is Artemis of Ephesus,' I echo biblical words
shouted by devoted cities before their towers fell
Queen of the Beasts and Protector of the Walls,
citadel-crowned and adorned with honeybees,
Mother of the Highest Point, the Safest Place
You stroke the soft manes of lions, teeth still bloody,
and rest Your heels upon the backs of castrated bulls

Lady of All Things Wild, even in the desert You roam
Among darkened tombs and monoliths You wander,
between oases trailing dusty caravans
golden lion, sand cat, tearer of flesh
Hatshepsut called You Pakhet,
watching over her daughter as
You guard Your own kittens

Goddess of the Fire, Goddess of the Itching Skin
Goddess of the Foaming Mouth, Goddess of the Bite
Wearing vulpine pelt and Freedom's cap,
Thracians once addressed You as Bendis
In that land of witches and wild tribes,
You shine a blazing torch in each hand
to illuminate herbs that harm, hinder, or heal
In high boots and bearskin, You lead leaping
hares and walk the sky brightly as the Moon

Queen of Three Worlds who waits at the forked path
where all decisions give birth to future consequence,
the Mysteries gave You many names
Romans knew You as Diana, Hecate
and Proserpine standing side by side,
serpents in Your hair and
hounds at Your feet

Goddess of the Guiding Lights, Goddess of Roads,
Goddess of Gates, Goddess of the Funeral Rites

Artemis, daughter of gentle Leto and friend to noble Herakles,
they now honor You around the world and in varied ways
from Munich to Dublin to Prague to Antwerp to Ankara
from London to Barcelona to Paris to Naples to Athens
from Singapore to Bangkok to Tokyo to Rio to San Juan
from Sydney to Cape Town to Toronto to San Francisco
from Lisbon to Toledo to Calgary to Atlanta to Hatfield
from Minneapolis to Kalamazoo to Kingston to Istanbul
from Cambridge to Miami to Las Vegas to Denver to D.C.

from Eugene to Lombard to Leesburg to Baltimore to Buffalo
from Peabody to Portland to Durham to Albuquerque to Austin
Goddess of Lycia, Goddess of Arcadia,
Goddess of Siracusa, Goddess of Nemi
I ask for nothing but Your confidence

Goddess of the Appalachians, Goddess of the Apennines
Goddess of the Alpheios, Goddess of the Potomac

Cynthia, Melissa, Delia, Alexandria,

I thank You

(*dedicated to the New Alexandrians*)

Artemis

by Amanda Sioux Blake

The Virgin Huntress

When Artemis was young (some say three years old) her father Zeus wanted to give Her a gift. When He asked Her what She wanted, She responded along the lines of "I want to run wild and free with my dogs and nymphs in the woods forever and never, ever marry." Zeus was not able to deny Her anything, and He granted Her request.

Artemis is the twin sister of Apollon, and the daughter of Zeus and Leto, a Titan-Goddess who bestowed the power of camouflage and moving about unseen on the animals of the Earth. Hera, furious over Zeus's latest affair, forbade any country or land to give Leto refuge. She declared that Leto would not give birth anywhere on Earth. Leto was very pregnant by now, and the birth could not help but come soon. She wandered the Earth and besought all the lands, kingdoms and city-states to give Her a place to rest, but all the rulers (as well as the rest of the populace) were too afraid of Hera's wrath to allow Her to give birth in their countries. Many felt sorry for Leto, but none dared challenge Hera.

Finally She reached Delos. At this time in history it was a floating island, not anchored to the bottom of the sea, and therefore did not count as 'real' land. There was no one living there to fear Hera, and the spirit of the island itself let Leto stay after She promised that it would become a sacred site for Her children's worshipers. Hera had another trick up Her sleeve, however. The Queen of the Gods tried to detain Her daughter Eileithyia, the Goddess of Childbirth, to prevent Leto from going into labor. But the other Goddesses intervened and snuck Eileithyia away, enabling Leto to give birth. No sooner was Artemis out herself than she helped her mother give birth to her twin brother Apollon, which shows that she was a Goddess of midwifery and helper of women in childbirth right from the start.

Although all animals are under Her protection, Her most sacred animals are commonly known to be bears, deer, and boars. Birds close to Her heart are buzzard-hawks and partridges. Her trees were palm and cypress, and Her holy flower was a red amaranth. The asphodel plant, a gray herb, was sometimes considered sacred to Her, especially when connected with Hekate. It was used for animal feed and connected with the underworld, and therefore sacred to both Persephone and Hekate. Artemis was often said to have been brought up alongside Demeter's daughter Kore/Persephone and the woodland nymphs, spending their time playing, gathering flowers, and mock fighting.

The metal silver is considered sacred to Her, most likely because silver is the color of the moon. She is depicted as having silver sandals, bows and arrows, and was identified with Selene, Goddess of the Moon, and Hekate, Goddess of Witchcraft, ghosts, and the dark moon; so much so that at times, Hekate was called the Khthonic (Underworld) Artemis. The identification with Selene came later, and the Triad of Artemis-Selene-Hekate that Wiccans usually refer to came from the Roman Era, instead of being the "original" form of the Goddess.

She spent most of Her time roaming mountain forests and untamed land with her nymphs hunting for lions, panthers, hinds and stags. Although She hunted the animals, She was also responsible for their safety and wellbeing; many early paintings of Artemis show Her in her capacity as Queen of the Wild Beasts (Potnia Theron), predators and prey alike eating from Her hands.

As a Goddess of wilderness, She protected the woods as a whole, but was sometimes considered a protector of the lakes and springs within them as well. She was called Limnaia or Limnaie, meaning "Lady of the Lake." Artemis' association with the natural world, the wilderness, can be easily seen to symbolize

Her own spirit. It was said "Zeus has made you [Artemis] a lion among women," again referring to Her independent nature.

She roams the forests in Her role as huntress and protectress. But She is related to childbirth as well. She eases the labor pains of human and animal alike and protects the young. It was said that when she was born, she caused her mother no pain. Whereas Eileithyia is the patron of mothers in childbirth, Artemis was the protector of the infant. She protected the young child of either gender, but remained the patron of girls until they married (and therefore entered the domain of Hera).

Being a protector of girls and women, She was also, perhaps in contradiction, their destroyer. It was believed that Artemis brought sudden death to infants, girls and women. Apollon possessed a similar role, bringing sudden death, illness and disease to boys and men. In an age where sex for a woman often could mean a death in childbirth, it is not hard to see how Artemis, whose power was in part associated with Her virginity, would be seen as the punishing or executing Goddess. Countering her role as death-dealer, Artemis was also regarded as not only the protector of young girls, but a Goddess of healing in her own right, like her brother.

Artemis is also called the Goddess of Maiden Dance and Song, which refers to the choral dances and rituals that only young women were allowed to enact. Artemis is said to lead the dances of the Muses and the Kharites (Graces) when on Mount Olympus. Artemis is attended by eighty nymphs; Okeanides, cloud nymphs and Naiads (freshwater nymphs). In Arkadian Stymphalos Artemis was attended by bird-legged nymphs, similar in appearance to the harpies, who also looked after her Arkadian temples.

As previously mentioned, Artemis was the protector of young girls until they married. Her twin brother Apollon fulfilled the complementary role for young boys. As the sister of Apollon, she is the bringer of light and wisdom to young girls as Apollon is to boys. Artemis and Apollon, although in many ways opposites

(Apollon is a solar/civilization deity, Artemis is a lunar/wilderness deity; Artemis is female, Apollon is male; Artemis is virgin, Apollon has many lovers of both sexes) they complement each other perfectly. Apollon is really the only male who is allowed into Artemis' inner circle. They work together well when they have a common cause. Both are extremely protective of their mother Leto, as the cautionary tale of the Niobids shows.

Avengers of Leto: The Niobids

Niobe was a Queen of Thebes, and she was excessively proud, especially of her fourteen children, seven boys and seven girls. One day the women of Thebes went to the temple of Leto to burn incense at her altars and pray to her as the patron of mothers. Niobe came to the temple where the rest of the Theban women were and asked:

"What madness makes you worship Gods you have merely heard about more highly then those you have seen? Why is Leto worshiped with altars, while my divine majesty receives no incense? My beauty is worthy of a Goddess, and I have seven daughters and seven sons, and I shall soon have sons-in-law and daughters-in-law. Leto gave birth to only two children, only one seventh the number of my offspring. I am blessed – for who can deny it? And I shall always be blessed – who can doubt it? The wealth of my blessings have made me safe, and I am above the reach of Fortune's arm."

Niobe then ordered the women to leave the temple and to cease worshiping Leto. The women obeyed their Queen and left, although Ovid makes it quite clear that they still worshiped Leto in their hearts, in silent devotion.

Leto was, of course, greatly offended. She complained to her children, and Apollon took up his bow and arrow and killed all seven of Niobe's sons as punishment. Her husband, Amphion, killed himself by driving a dagger into his heart when he heard the news. Perhaps Leto and Apollon thought that Niobe would see the error of her ways and repent her crime, and live the rest of her days with her daughters. This, however, was not to be.

Even the death of her sons did not faze the cold-hearted Queen of Thebes. As the prideful Niobe bent over the body of her sons, she cried to the heavens "Even in my misery I have more left to me then you have in your glory. Even after so many deaths I am the victor!"

No sooner had she spoken those foolish words then Artemis took her bow and shot down Niobe's daughters, her only remaining children. Niobe in her grief was turned to stone. The stone still weeps, but never moves.

Artemis : Protector of Girlhood

Artemis is the protector of the young girl-child and the preteen girl, up until the time that she is married and becomes Hera's responsibility. When a girl of Athens married, she took her toys and children's clothes and left them on the altar of Artemis, along with locks of her hair, thereby leaving behind childhood and becoming a woman.

One of the most intriguing rituals performed for Artemis was the *arkteia*, 'bear-service,' played out by young Athenian girls. Pausanias says that all girls were required to "act the bear" for Artemis before marriage. Lillan E. Doherty, the author of *Gender and the Interpretation of Classical Myth*, points out that:

"The range of the girls' ages is still debated, but they were all unmarried, some apparently as young as five....While some adults are portrayed wearing bear-masks in the vase fragments from Brauron, the girls to not dress as bears; they are shown racing, sometimes in the nude, and dancing or walking in procession. The ages of the girls and their activities suggest some form of initiation rite."

Doherty goes on to suggest that in acting the bear for Artemis, the girls acted out the wildness and aggression that they would have to repress when they married and were expected to become obedient wives. Greek society seemed to have regarded young girls as a naturally wild force that must be reckoned with, and eventually, tamed for the good of society, in order to make them into docile wives and mothers.

Artemis and Aktaion

Artemis is the fierce and wild protector of virginity. Although She was often a gentle and nurturing Goddess to women and animals, let any man try to force his way into Her presence and he would be punished severely. The hunter Aktaion learned this the hard way. One night, while wandering the wilds, he came upon Artemis and her nymphs, who were bathing in a pool after a long day of hunting. The fool should have turned around and run for his life when he realized it was the virgin Goddess of the hunt. But he stood, enraptured, transfixed, and gazed open-mouthed at the beautiful, naked Artemis and her likewise bare attendants

It was Her nymphs who first noticed him; the Naiads shrieked and tried to cover themselves. Artemis rose from the bath, pearly white flesh glistening, her eyes darkened and terrible to behold, furious with the insolent mortal for gawking at Her and Her girls, for violating this sacred female-only sanctuary. To punish him, She turned Aktaion into a stag; the very animal he was hunting that night. His own hunting dogs, not recognizing him, leaped upon him and tore him to pieces.

Artemis and Prokis

Despite the violence visited upon the unwelcome intruder into Her sacred woods, Artemis did not always punish Her nymphs or mortal hunting companions if they fell in love or decided to marry. If the nymph or mortal woman was upfront with Artemis, she was allowed to leave Her followers on good terms. It was when one of Her attendants lied and attempted to cover up her affair that Artemis became angry, for only virgins were allowed in the holy circle of her hunting companions.

The tale of Prokis is not a well-known story, but shows an interesting side of Artemis. Prokris was a hunting companion of Artemis in her girlhood, but when she fell in love with King Kephalos of Krete she left the attendants of Artemis to marry him. Several years later, however, she discovered that her husband was having an affair with Eos, the Goddess of the Dawn. Upset, she ran away from Krete and into Artemis's sacred groves to find her old friend. At first, Artemis told her that since she wasn't a virgin anymore she couldn't hunt with her. But when Prokris told Artemis what had happened and about her husband's infidelity, the Goddess felt pity for her old friend and decided to help her. In what was probably the only time that Artemis played matchmaker, She devised a plan to help Prokris win back her husband. First, since Kephalos was an avid hunter, She gave Prokris two gifts to give to him: a javelin that never missed its mark, and Laelaps, an excellent hunting dog who no wild beast could escape.

Then, Artemis cut Prokris' hair and dressed her like a boy, so her husband would not recognize her. Under Artemis' instruction, she then went to Kephalos and challenged him. She beat him in hunting, killing many more animals than him. When Kephalos saw that the javelin and the dog were so great he wanted them badly. He asked the stranger to sell them to him. She refused. He promised to give the stranger half his kingdom; she still refused. He then asked her what it what it was that "he" wanted. She said that the King could only have them if he slept with her. The King wanted the javelin and the dog so bad that, still thinking that she was a boy, he agreed. When they came to the bedroom in the King's palace, Prokris took off the boy's clothes and showed her husband that she was a woman and his runaway wife. After that, she was again in his favor.

Artemis and the House of Atreus

Agamemnon was the King of Mycenae and the brother of Helen of Sparta's (later Helen of Troy) original husband. The House of Atreus was an accursed house. The deck was already stacked against Agamemnon and his kin. But his foolishness and hubris led to his death and that of his wife and daughter.

Artemis was extremely possessive. She would punish anyone who killed Her sacred animals. Agamemnon incited Her wrath when he killed a stag in one of her groves. To add insult to injury, upon shooting it he declared that Artemis herself could not have made a better shot!

While on their way to Troy the Spartan and Mycenaean fleet was becalmed at Aulis. With no wind, the ships were dead in the water. Agamemnon consulted the seer Kalkhos, who had been brought with the fleet. Kalkhos told him that the Goddess Artemis was angry with him, and that ships would not sail on to Troy until he sacrificed his daughter Iphigenia. Agamemnon sent word to his wife to send the girl, saying that she was going to marry the famed hero Akhilleus. When poor Iphigenia got there, of course, she found that she was not going to her wedding but to her death. After she was dead, the ships were able to sail on to Troy.

The civilized Greeks could scarcely stomach the idea of human sacrifice at all, let alone a father sacrificing his own daughter. Euripides made it easier for the Greek conscience by saying that at the last possible moment Artemis whisked the girl off to be her priestess and a deer was substituted in her place instead.

But it did not save Agamemnon. His daughter was gone. And by the time the Trojan War was over, word had reached his homeland of his plans to sacrifice her. He sailed home to find that his wife was none too forgiving. She, along with her lover, killed him and took over rule of his kingdom.

And so the play *Orestes* begins. Orestes is the unfortunate brother of Iphigenia, who now finds himself duty-bound, commanded by the God Apollon who embodies reason and the social order and who is incidentally Artemis' twin brother, to avenge the murder of his father Agamemnon. Yet he knows that if he kills his mother Clytemnestra, he will be haunted by the Furies, ancient Goddesses who torment criminals. Crimes against blood-kin are the worst possible, and these ancient matriarchal Goddesses considered the murder of a mother especially heinous. Poor Orestes is damned if he does and damned if he doesn't.

Artemis and Sacrifice

I have always experienced Artemis as a nurturing influence in my life. Although violent when provoked to protect those who cannot protect themselves or to defend the sacred solitude of her groves as a retreat from civilization, I do not see Her as an inherently bloodthirsty Goddess. How, then, do we reconcile this gentle experience of Artemis with the story of the sacrifice of Iphigenia? Why would Artemis demand the life of an innocent girl to punish the father?

In Tauri, Artemis was said to regularly receive human sacrifices. The Taurians appear to have been considered primitive and warlike by the mainland Greeks, a "barbarian" tribe. There is no archaeological evidence for actual human sacrifice in the cults of Artemis. Although it is conceivable that human sacrifice may have been practiced in some far-distant archaic past, it is doubtful that we would have no archaeological evidence of it whatsoever. Artemis receiving human sacrifice is likely to be the invention of myth. It is always attributed to "barbarians" outside of Greece, and therefore the known world and civilization.

If human sacrifice is an invention of myth, then it still speaks of an aspect of the Goddess, so let us examine it. In mythology, death is not always literal. Many times it symbolizes an extreme transformation from one state to another, a shift in being that cannot be undone. Apollon presides over the entry of young boys into manhood, complementary to Artemis's role with girls, and his myths are filled with this symbolic death of youths. Hyakinthos, a lover of Apollon who died in a sporting accident involving a discus was transformed into the hyacinth flower. Cyparissus, a later love of Apollon, had a pet stag that he loved very much. One day he accidentally pierced its heart with his javelin, killing his beloved pet. He begged to be able to mourn his stag forever, and so Apollon turned him into the cypress tree, the tree of mourning, saying "I shall mourn for you, for others you shall mourn; you [the cypress tree] shall attend when men with grief are torn."

On Artemis' Worship Today

Modern society can be deadening to the soul. The vicious maneuvering and backstabbing of corporate boardrooms; the glossy magazine ads telling you you're not good enough as you are; pounding, throbbing music with violent, misogynistic lyrics; aggressive marketing urging you to buy more junk you don't need; the pressure to spend long hours at the office in the endless pursuit of the almighty dollar; government lies; 24-hour news channels bringing you more reports of murders, rapes, wars. It's enough to put you into a near-catatonic state of cynicism and depression. Hearing the quiet voice of Nature can be all but impossible in the never-ending racket of Western culture.

Artemis teaches you where to draw the line, how to separate the sacred groves of your inner self from the "civilized" world outside, and to tend to and nurture the child within. If need be, She teaches you to defend yourself, your sacred space, from the onslaught of intruders who would violate the land, to refuse to allow the media to dictate your self-image, or your boss to convince you to work longer hours instead of spending the time with your family. She teaches you to say "No. That's mine." Artemis helps you keep that little patch of wildness in your soul that you need to keep your sanity in the concrete jungles of modern life.

Artemis

by Kenn Payne

Hounds bay at the new moon,
Curved like the bow that She wields.
Clouds like pearlescent wraiths
Move softly overhead.
The night breeze bares the scent
Of jasmine.
A deer leaps!
An arrow flies!
And in the dark a creature dies.
Blood –
Like khthonic quicksilver
In the shadows,
Wells into a deep and true wound.
The Huntress: strong and fair
Eternal maiden, the bear.
Shining savior, women's protector
Claims the trophy with pride in Her eyes.

The Virgin Goddess

by Thista Minai

In ancient Greece, Artemis was known as a virgin Goddess. Today, as modern Hellenes attempt to revive ancient Greek religion and apply it to the modern world, we must reassess the meaning of Artemis's virginity, and attempt to understand why She chose this state.

It's important to clarify that 'virginity' was a very different thing in ancient Greece than it is for us in the modern world. To them, sexual abstinence was an after effect of virginity, *not* the definition of the word. The ancient Greeks did not believe the hymen existed, and virgin births were a regular occurrence rather than a rare miracle (see Giulia Sissa's *Greek Virginity*). *Parthenos* is the Greek word that generally gets translated as "virgin." Determining what it actually meant to be a *parthenos* is incredibly complicated, and one is likely to come up with a different answer for every polis. Luckily for Hellenes and modern scholars, the vast majority of what we know of ancient Greek myth and culture comes from Athens. Furthermore, the other Greek city-states were tremendously influenced by Athens due to its early victory over Persia and its subsequent financial and cultural success. So, while what we conclude about ancient Greek virgins based on Athenian social structure might not apply to all city-states (Sparta being the classic example), it will hold true for most of them, and will be at least relevant to all of them.

So what did it mean to be an Athenian *parthenos*? Ideally it meant an unmarried young woman who still lived with her father and never had sex. Athenian men wanted to ensure that their wives would bear legitimate heirs, so daughters were kept under strict supervision and seclusion to ensure that they had not been exposed to any other men before meeting their husbands. The one interesting exception was at certain festivals for Artemis, where unmarried women performed dances that the men watched, and this was often men's only opportunity to see their future brides.

There are many situations in which this ideal wasn't quite the same as the reality. Lower class families, for example, often couldn't afford to have their daughters spinning and weaving in seclusion, and so these young women would work the land with the rest of the family. However, even these women were still supposed to remain virgins. In the cases where a young woman *did* have sex, that did not necessarily end her *parthenia*, or virginity. Sissa writes, "Penetration by a male organ deflowered a virgin, yet the event existed only if it was found out by family and society or revealed by its consequences: the parthenic state depended on sexuality, hence on the body, yet was also a purely negative fact." Thus, if no one knew a woman had sex, she was still a *parthenos*, in contrast to the modern idea where once you've had sex, you're no longer a virgin, regardless of whether or not other people know about it. Unmarried women who managed to conceal a pregnancy, were allowed to give birth under other strange circumstances (usually only applicable in myth), or who bore a child without anyone having discovered the circumstances under which the child was conceived, were said to have had a 'virgin birth', and their sons were known as *partheniai*, or sons of virgins (Sissa, **Greek Virginity**, 79-83).

All these details considered, the fact remains that the ideal *parthenos* was a virgin in the modern sense of the word. Men wanted to know their children would be theirs, and not sired by some other man their wife had lain with in secret. If we keep in mind the fact that almost all ancient Greek myths we have to study today were written by men, and that the Greeks believed their Gods, especially the Olympians, to be perfect – that is, they embodied ideals – then we can assume that the variety of *parthenia* intended in the myths of Artemis we are familiar with would be the Athenian man's ideal model of a *parthenos*. Therefore, according to ancient Greek myth, Artemis doesn't have sex, never has, and never will.

Assuming that ancient Greek myth is valuable to modern Hellenism despite the overwhelmingly male point of view from which it was written, the important question becomes why. Why would Artemis choose to be a virgin? She asked Zeus of Her own will to remain a *parthenos* forever, so there must be some reason that She desired to abstain from sex and marriage. What is that reason?

The answer to this question can be found by studying the oracle of Apollo at Delphi. The Pythia was a virgin priestess of Apollo who gave prophecies from the God in His temple at Delphi. Sissa tells us (again in *Greek Virginity*) that vapors coming from a crack in the earth induced a hallucinogenic trance in which the Pythia delivered these oracles. The fumes entered the Pythia's vagina as she sat on a tripod perched over the chasm. Sissa goes on to explain how the significance of this lies in the ancient Greek perception of symmetry in the human body: the ancient Greeks believed the body to be symmetrical not only horizontally, but vertically as well. Thus the vagina and the mouth corresponded to one another. Therefore, when the essence of Apollo, in the form of fumes emitted from the earth, entered the Pythia through her vagina, it was logical to the ancient Greeks that this essence would then exit her body through her mouth in the form of divine prophecies. In order for the Greeks to be absolutely certain that all the words escaping her lips were sent by the God Himself and only Him, the Pythia must be completely pure and devoid of outside influences, i.e., chaste. In this way the authenticity of her oracles were guaranteed, because the only things coming out of her mouth were the same things that went into her 'mouth.'

The implications of this are tremendous. This relationship between Apollo and His priestess echoes a widely held belief about ancient Greek women and their husbands: Not only did a woman belong to her husband, but his essence permeated her. His influence entered her during sex, and so every word she spoke was his word channeled through her. This basic concept also applies to the ancient Greek understanding of men and women in general. Men were considered purely projective (as their penis spews forth their essence, so must their mouths when we apply vertical symmetry) and women were considered purely receptive. Furthermore, a woman's individuality is somehow contaminated by a man's spirit during intercourse. Once he spills his essence into her, everything she says and does has his essence in it.

This is where we find the reason behind Artemis' virginity. As a Goddess of both freedom, independence, and the untouched purity of wild nature, Artemis must preserve an identity that is completely uninfluenced by any other being. She could not allow anyone else to cloud Her individuality. The ancient Greeks believed that the only way for a woman (or Goddess, in this case) to remain purely Herself and not have Her identity influenced by anyone else was to abstain from sex. In the minds of the ancient Greek men who wrote down the myths we are now familiar with, the only acceptable way for Artemis to avoid intercourse permanently was to remain a *parthenos* eternally, and thus never be bound by the responsibilities of a wife to bear children.

To take all this information one step further and ask how Artemis would manifest Herself in modern society, or if She would still require Her followers to be virgins today (as they were in ancient Greece), is effectively unsolvable. The answer would be dependent not only on the individual person in question, but also on their personal approach to reconstructing ancient Greek religion. For example, for a woman determined to be as authentic to ancient Greek culture as possible in every aspect of their worship, perhaps they would need to abstain from sex with men. Having sex with women is arguably acceptable, for if this woman is working with the ancient Greek understanding of men and women, then two women, both being purely receptive beings, are incapable of contaminating each other's identities. If this were a man instead, the answer might be entirely different. Perhaps they could have sex freely without needing to worry about contamination of their identity, for if men are only projective, then they have no receptiveness with which to receive the identity of another. However, one could also look at the myth of Hippolytos and assume that virginity is the best way to stay close to Artemis regardless of one's own gender, although I would caution anyone determined to abstain entirely from sex, and suggest they take a good look at what ultimately happened to Hippolytos and why. On the other hand, this same question could yield a very different answer for someone who wishes to use a modern understanding of gender and sex. Perhaps sex is less binding to them, and it is instead relationships which have an unquestionable influence on their independence and individuality, or perhaps they are one of those rare and unique people who can keep their individuality and freedom in tact while being romantically or sexually involved with someone. The point is that there is no longer a set rule in this matter. In the modern world, each individual who wishes to be closer to Artemis must approach Her and discover which path is right for them.

The Fertile Goddess

by Thista Minai

Since writing *The Virgin Goddess* I have continued to ponder the nature of Artemis' virginity. While I can look at Artemis Parthenos through the lens of ancient Greek culture and neatly understand Her virginity as a symbol for untouched nature and untainted independence, there are certain elements of this expression of the independent ideal that clash with other aspects of Artemis' nature. How does the Virgin become the Goddess of Childbirth? While ancient Greek culture is filled with contradictions, they generally end up being two sides of the same coin. Hermes, for example, is both messenger and liar because He is a God of language, and words can be used to articulate both truth and fiction. Artemis the Huntress also protects animals because if She does not, soon there will be no animals left to hunt; as Goddess of women She can both save the life of a woman in peril and grant her a swift death. Everywhere there seems to be contradiction there is balance beneath the surface. The virgin and the nurturer, however, never seemed to find that balance in my mind. I could not understand what connection there might be between the sterile virgin who loved no one and the caring mother to the young of all species.

Then, entirely by chance, I stumbled upon an old book that pointed out something so obvious I laughed out loud at myself for never realizing it before. In *The Cults of the Greek States*, Lewis Richard Farnell points out that Artemis was never actually worshipped as a virgin in ancient Greek cult practice. While the concept of Artemis as a virgin does appear quite early, it is purely literary, occurring only in hymns and myths. There was "no public worship of Artemis the chaste." (p. 444) While I certainly do not agree with everything Farnell has written, some quick cross checking revealed he was absolutely right in this case. Furthermore, as Farnell points out, Artemis' cult representations were often thick with fertility and occasionally, as in the case of the *lombai* (Hesych. s.v. *lombai*), allude to sexual activity.

If Artemis, then, was not a virgin in cult, why was the image of Artemis the Virgin so important to ancient Greek myth and literature? I believe there are many sides to this issue. To begin with, as I described in *The Virgin Goddess*, male-dominated ancient Greek society had some very powerful ideas (which may seem rather peculiar or downright offensive to us today) about what women were, how they were supposed to act, and why that was. Looking at the female body from the ancient Greek perspective, a woman who partook in sexual activity could never be purely herself; she was inevitably tainted by the essence of the man she slept with. A Goddess of nature had to be as pure as the wilderness itself; therefore She must be a virgin, and the only acceptable way for a woman to remain a virgin would be to obtain permission from her father to remain *parthenos* forever (which we see in Callimachus *Hymn* III).

The important thing to notice here is that all these myths were written (or at least recorded) by men. This was the male perspective on how Artemis presented Herself. This is, of course, not to say that there is no worth or validity in the male perspective. To the contrary, there is something wholly enchanting about the Virgin Huntress that has captivated us for thousands of years. She is the nature we can never see because the moment we step foot in it, it is no longer pure, and yet the pursuit of such wild freedom can be wholly engrossing. Only by becoming that wilderness ourselves can we ever reach it, and then we are forever changed. The cold yet joyous virgin huntress is an invaluable and undeniably true symbol for the pursuit of wildness, freedom, and independence within our selves.

This wild, austere ideal may not have been an exclusively male perspective, however what literary fragments we have from female ancient Greek writers are sparse and thus would not make well founded conclusions. Either way, what evidence we have does show that Artemis the Virgin was a purely literary manifestation, perhaps because it expresses an intellectual ideal rather than a visceral reality. This does not mean we should give up the chase, but rather that the fertile Goddess of Nature shows us a wholly different side of Artemis that was better expressed through cult.

The surface of ancient Greek cult seems to echo the images of mythology: Artemis the virgin goddess could only be served by virgin priestesses. This, however, is just as deeply infused with the ancient Greek male perspective as the mythological ideal itself. A priestess of Artemis was supposed to be a representative of the Goddess Herself, almost a sort of walking, talking image. She would have to do everything she could to be as much like Artemis as possible, and thus would have had to abstain from sex for the same reasons as Artemis: she too must maintain a purity of essence by remaining untainted by the essence of a man. The priestess, then, is a sort of living illustration of Artemis. One must note, however, that these priestesses were never life-long servants of Artemis (Connelly, *Portrait of a Priestess*, p.18). The ancient Greeks believed it was unacceptable for a respectable woman to remain a *parthenos* indefinitely. A virgin could serve a limited term as a priestess of Artemis, but when the term ended she was expected to move on; marriage was inevitable. Only the mythological Iphigenia was thought to have served her whole life in service of Artemis as a virgin priestess, but she is a part of literature, not cult. No ancient Greek woman ever served Artemis as a virgin priestess for her entire life.

While a priestess of Artemis was certainly a virgin, Her worshippers were just as often mothers as they were unmarried girls. In myth Her companions were always virgins, but this is not an accurate representation of the types of women who actually came to pray in Her temples, nor is the mythological ideal of the Virgin Huntress an accurate representation of the Goddess they prayed to. Virgin women danced in honor of Artemis at certain festivals as a way to show off for potential husbands (Burkert, *Greek Religion*, p.151), girls dancing the *arkteia* in Attica were thought to be preparing for marriage, pregnant women prayed to Artemis for help in childbirth, and Euripides tells us that Artemis Lokhia would not speak to childless women at all (Euripides, *Suppliants*, 955). Here we see Artemis presiding over preparation for marriage, pregnancy, and childbirth, and considering this along with Artemis' obvious associations with nature, wilderness, and both wild and domestic animals (which images and votives confirm were part of cult as well as myth), a connection with the eminently fertile Goddess of Ephesos is not so strange.

All this taken into account, how important is virginity to a follower of Artemis after all? In light of all we have seen here, it's not very important at all. Even in ancient Greece women who loved and prayed to Artemis were not always virgins. Any woman who wants to understand the essence of her own self, or who wants to experience wild freedom, or who wants to be blessed with fertility and healthy children can find an aspect of Artemis to worship joyfully.

Modern priestesses of Artemis might also find that virginity is not so important, but the image of virginity is – that essence of purity and independence is essential to Artemis' character, but without ancient Greek notions concerning the bodies and natures of women and men, sexual abstinence becomes far less important. It is the sense of wild independence that is so necessary, and a modern woman can achieve this state of being in many different ways. We are no longer bound to the cultural concepts of ancient Greek society. Consequently we may also find that ancient Greek priestesses are not particularly good role models for modern priestesses after all. Ancient priesthoods were often just as political as spiritual, if not more so, and were occasionally bought. In this and countless other ways the very meaning of priesthood has changed since ancient times, and now we must reevaluate what we want our clergy to be, or what we feel a priest or priestess ought to provide. We cannot expect a modern priestess of Artemis to be just like the priestesses of antiquity.

Today the Artemis we actively worship and work with need not be a Virgin Goddess. The mythological Virgin can and should still haunt our dreams, challenging us to a purity of being that will lead us to a deep understanding of our own nature, but the Artemis we physically interact with at our home shrines, during a stroll in the forest, in a corner of our garden – this Goddess can be something entirely different, something fertile and nurturing and even motherly. Sexual virginity may not be significant to a modern perspective on Artemis, but independence is important, and is in fact essential to one being an effective mother. Here we finally see the connection between the virgin and the nurturer – the mother hears no call louder than that of her young and thus must remain in a way untouchable to other affections. When need arises, her children come first and foremost.

The many manifestations of Artemis call to deep parts of our soul. She can be an inspiration for single working mothers who provide for their children on their own, for proud feminists fighting for women's rights, for men who love and respect the wilderness, and for happily married couples who celebrate the wildness within themselves. We do not need to emulate Her to welcome Her into our lives (which is not to say that one shouldn't, merely that it is not required), nor do modern women need to push themselves into an ancient mold to serve Her. Any woman who has the courage to respond to the call of her own heart despite what anyone else might say about it, married or single, mother or childless, virgin or not, is beloved of Artemis.

Artemis Speaks

by Melia Suez

Run with me
Before me
Or behind.
Just run
And laugh
And dance.
Call on me, speak with me
Look to the moon to feel my love.
Tread the paths, high and low.
Lover, sister, friend, mistress.
Feel my symbol on your brow
Wear my symbol on your chest
Move child
Run, laugh, dance.
With or without fear.
Hound, deer and hawk
I've sent your way
Bow, arrow and moon
What more do you need
To see my wish for you
Honor me, love me.
Run with me
Before me
Or Behind.
Laugh and dance.

Artemis of the Ephesians

by Corbin

Goddess of the greatest temple, you who keep
All desires banished in the circles of your deep
Eternal ocean, from which all things are born,
To which all things in time give up their form:
What mortal mind can hope to comprehend
Even the questions to which you are the answer?
The shrine they built you long ago in Ephesus,
That perfect form of stone, immense and glorious,
The like of which was never seen but on Olympus,
Has vanished now with all its storied age to dust.
Lost is the city above the shining harbor
Where gliding ships from many ports came to anchor
And caravans marched down from the high interior,
Bearing the wealth of all the world to the Mother.
Fabrics and fine wood, incense, ivory and gold:
All offered as gifts to the Mother of the World.
And oh! the shimmering morning of your holy day,
Flutes and rattles shrilling along the sacred way
Princes, merchants, beggars, priests jostling to see
Your appearance at the portal of epiphany.
Your statue that fell from heaven on a moonless night,
Face and hands shiny black and thirty breasts of white,
With wingéd bulls and lions clinging to your gown,
The necklace of the Zodiac and the woven spiral crown.
Your worship even that bully Paul could not outface*
With his arrogant preaching in the marketplace
Till the jeers and stones of your people made him fly:
Who does not know our Goddess and her image that fell
    from the sky?
But all has been forgotten now, by all except we few
Who seek to rekindle your worship, relearn the true
Rites of reverence by which the Earth revolves

In whatever time remains before our age dissolves
Into your circling ocean, from which all things are born,
To which all things in time give up their form.

* See *Acts of the Apostles*, 19:23-36.

Invocations of Artemis

by Rebecca Buchanan

i. Artemis Wild Virgin

The salt sea is not so silver,
nor the lily so pure,
nor midnight so deep
as the wild Virgin.

ii. Wild Artemis

Goddess of wild green
of rushing streams
of birth-bed blood
Goddess of steep mountains
of stinging swamps
of roaring coasts
Artemis

iii. Terrible one

O Terrible One
Who hunts me in the darkness,
Driving me on before Your hounds
Laughing ...
Your eyes glow with holy silver light
Your voice is like the frost, icy clear and pure,
Driving on Your baying hounds in their wild hunt
Through dark woodland of nightmare horrors --
sharp-toothed and deep-eyed
Laughing ...

iv. Forest Lady

Forest Lady:
May the rocks which are Your bones be strong and solid;

May the streams which are Your blood flow clean and pure:
May the grass which is Your coat grow thick and green;
May the trees which are Your antlers stand tall and majestic;
May the flowers which are Your eyes bloom bright and colorful.
Lady, may Your Forest-Self be always a place of beauty and life.

v. Huntress

Muses
Sing of Artemis
Deer Slayer
Swift-footed
Strong-thighed
Great Voiced
Who delights in the chase
– over shadowy hills
and windy peaks
through forests
dense and green
Sending out fatal shafts

The tangled wood
echoes with the
death cries of beasts –

And you dance with cheerful heart

vi. Stern-eyed

Artemis
Stern-eyed
Your brother declares the will of Zeus
But it is you who enforces it
With arrows swift and true

My Life with Artemis

by Lupa

Sometimes the most important relationships with deities, spirits and other beings are the ones we aren't even aware are happening. While some people are fortunate enough to develop an innate sense for the spiritual early on in life, and are encouraged to turn imagination-with-a-small-i into Imagination-with-a-big-I, others start out mostly blind and deaf to the spiritual. Or, as in my case, they end up so discouraged from anything even remotely "strange" that there was no context to compare potentially spiritual experiences to.

I was one of those kids who was constantly grubbing around in the woods, catching garter snakes, and being absolutely fascinated by monarch butterflies coming to form in delicate chrysalises. Also being of a bookish bent, I devoured everything the library had on animals and nature. I could rattle off random biological factoids, and often did to the amusement of the neighbors. There were plenty of pets during my childhood as well.

All of this was well and good. However, there were other aspects to my interests that were strictly not talked about; I almost instinctually knew that they were taboo. For example, I told no one that I walked around our front yard talking to listeners I couldn't see, but was pretty sure were there. And for the longest time, there was a part of me that identified more as a wolf than as a human being, and felt that I'd been born in the wrong body.

And then there was the rather unfortunate matter that I simply wasn't like the other girls in my school. Well into my teens I preferred the company of the wilderness, and only stopped spending every day in the woods behind the house the day I came home to find them bulldozed to make way for a new housing development. I also stubbornly refused to wear cosmetics or dress up, and was often told to "do something with your hair, already!" And there were always the animals, too, a constant presence in one form or another. With shocking traits like that, who would dare to bring up "feeling" presences, or wanting to howl at the moon?

So I muddled through adolescence, bearing the sin of unpopularity, and continuing to find covert ways to express myself, and things I didn't entirely understand.

Enter Artemis

When I was seventeen, I made friends with the closest thing my small town had to a pagan community at the time – a group of folks about my age who were interested in various forms of paganism, goth subculture, and White Wolf roleplaying games. The internet was still relatively new outside of the most cutting edges of geekery, and being in a small town hadn't helped me with getting access. Still, these folks had smatterings of information that, for the first time, made me realize that I wasn't entirely alone in my "overactive imagination." Maybe there were reasons for odd feelings and interests after all.

I'll spare you the details of awkward beginnings and a bit of young love. Suffice it to say that by the time February of 1998 rolled around, I was somewhat more experienced in the wonders of eclectic paganism, was still living at home to be able to get through college without student loans, and was nearing the end of a two and a half year relationship that had gone rather on the sour side. I was still nominally Catholic, though I'd been studying paganism and magical practice (and dabbling in the latter in a sorta-Christian kind of way) for the past few years.

On the evening of 8 February, 1998, I came home after a night out with my then-boyfriend. The moon was nearing full, and her light streamed into the windows. And then I had the sudden urge – to dance. I had never danced before. I had always been that one at the school dances who sat on the sidelines, scared to go out there. I had been so out of touch with what was popular I didn't even recognize the music. And I was terribly self-conscious, so the concept of dancing was alien to me. Yet there, alone in the moonlight, I danced, and I danced freeform. Back and forth around the bed I danced, exulting in the beauty of the light, the feeling of my graceful body, the sheer joy of not giving a damn what anyone thought. And in that moment Artemis made herself known to me, and told me I was hers.

I don't remember what she told me, exactly. But from that moment on, I began to change. I became more independent and self-assertive. I became more bold in my relationships. I stopped hemming and hawing about paganism, and decided to just dive on in. And over the next decade I would do my best to emulate this goddess I admired so much, and who taught me a lot just through her example.

Daughter of the Huntress

What I hadn't really caught on to, and wouldn't realize for some time, was that I already had been emulating Artemis, and that she'd already been a quiet but powerful influence in my life for many years. The more I learned about her and interacted with her, the more I saw where the attraction between us was.

The near-obsession with animals and the natural world was a no-brainer. And the same went for the independent streak I've always had, which manifested itself, among other things, as fiery feminism in my undergrad years. Left to my own devices, I think I might have delayed dating entirely, and would have been perfectly happy as an eternal maiden; I primarily started cultivating an interest in boys due to social pressure (though I'd found girls intriguing even in preadolescence).

There were certain things that I'd had an interest in that, due to circumstances beyond my control, I'd never had a chance to explore in much depth. Being raised by people who weren't particularly fond of the deep wilderness, I never had a chance to go camping, let alone hunting, as a child. (I never even went camping until I was in my twenties – I've worked to make up for lost time since then.) And that aforementioned sexual attraction to girls never even had a chance to manifest beyond a crush on a friend, thanks to a combination of Catholic family/religious community and local redneck conservatism.

I found all these traits reflected either in the lore about Artemis, or in my interactions with her. While I don't condone treating deities as archetypes that only exist in the collective unconscious, I do appreciate the concept of archetypes as common "templates" that deities and other beings may adhere to in a general capacity. I do believe that human beings also sometimes gravitate towards archetypal patterns as well, and as I studied the archetype of the virgin huntress I saw myself.

Sadly, society and repression had taken their toll. I never regained the innocence and focus of my youth, and even a decade spent with Artemis as my patron deity couldn't completely reverse the damage. I sometimes wonder if part of the reason she arrived when she did was to try and preserve what was left; that's one thing I've never asked her.

Transitions

My time with Artemis was rather unorthodox. I never even remotely resembled a Hellenic pagan. Our interactions were very informal, and the closest we got to formality was a ritual I would perform on February 8 of every year. It was rarely scripted, and sometimes consisted simply of a walk in the woods, conversing with the huntress. Other than that, Artemis mainly acted as a role model for me, helping to guide my everyday actions, and trying to regain some of the qualities we had shared earlier in my life, but which I had lost over time.

Sometimes she surprised me. Due to feminist rhetoric, I had become accustomed to Artemis being typified as a man-hater, and an opponent of marriage across the board. Yet as I grew older, and my relationships with men more serious (I never seemed to have the greatest luck with women, and in fact repressed my love of them for years), I started thinking of a lifelong commitment. I worked up the nerve to ask her for her opinion, worried that she might tell me to break things off after a certain point. Yet she informed me that men today were not the men of ancient Greece, and that while she hadn't always agreed with my choice of partners, she hadn't had reason to intervene.

It shouldn't have surprised me that, not too long after I got married, she chose to change the nature of our relationship in a dramatic fashion. She didn't choose to take a step back because I was married, but my life has a strong tendency towards synchronicities. Rather, a decade to the day after she made herself known to me, Artemis stepped aside to let someone else in.

I'd had fair warning. The year before, on our 9th anniversary, she told me that a male god would be coming into my life soon – she didn't tell me who, but she told me to prepare to work with him more closely. Not that she would go away entirely, but she would step back and let him take over for a while. And a year later, I said my farewells to her, and expressed my gratitude for all she had done for me.

Waiting

Someday, at some point down the line, Artemis will be back – or so she said. For now, I focus on my relationship with the god I've been working with since she left. Actually, "left" isn't the right term. She's still around; I still feel her presence. But it's not as strong. And I've changed as well, reflecting that shift in influence.

I don't think she'll ever leave, and I don't think she's ever not been here. My awareness of her may have changed over time, and probably will always be evolving as I grow and change and learn. But I'll await the time when she chooses to step back into my life, and see where that path takes us.

Artemis and the Modern Man

by Bronto Sproximo

"Muse, sing of Artemis, sister of the Far-shooter, the virgin who delights in arrows, who was fostered with Apollo" – *The Homeric Hymn 9 To Artemis*

Step forward you who would know the maiden huntress and celebrate those dedicated to meeting her expectations.

Those with a superficial knowledge of the gods have used words like "angry" or "man-hater" to describe Artemis. These are unfortunate and narrow-minded interpretations. Like her brother she has high expectations for humanity, especially in the treatment of women and children. Think on how frequently and crushingly disappointed she must be and the derivation of her aloofness will not be so mysterious.

The Spartans worshiped her, I would suggest, because her expectations where so high. The historical record is exhaustive in describing Lakonian shrines and temples of Artemis, especially Artemis Orthia. If the Spartan men felt they would be hated for their gender, why so much dedicated worship? Why the *diamastigosis* in her honor?

Artemis shunned the company of men and demanded her nymphs do the same. This was not out of a hatred of intercourse but a requirement for independence. In the era in which the myths were written heterosexual relations meant a woman was subservient to a man.

The goddess of independence could not allow herself to be subject to a male. The maiden goddess does not necessarily refer to her sexual innocence, but a statement that she was whole without needing a man to complete her. As regards those who marry, her expectation is that each should treat the other as a partner, that there should be no 'dependant.' If marriage in the ancient world meant the woman became the chattel of the man then a truly independent woman could not marry.

Hunters were independent: they could feed, clothe and defend themselves with the tools of their trade. The huntress aspect of Artemis represents this independence. As goddess of the wild places, she looks to protect the places where one can still go and be independent.

She has been called an angry goddess. I once saw two children laughing. The first started laughing for no reason at all. The second child heard the first child laughing and laughed too. For those minutes they were giggling for no reason at all with the overwhelming enthusiasm of innocent youth. In that moment I felt Artemis' presence and those children and I basked in her warmth and I felt the weight of adulthood lifted from me temporarily.

Although these two children likely lived their lives in safety and comfort, countless others do not. Whether the loss of innocence comes at the hands of one cruel adult or the inequality of society, the damage done to the innocent must enrage her, as it should all of us.

I sincerely believe that Artemis has special horrors in store for that offense.

The world can be a cruel place and although victims may have her sympathy, those with a victim mentality do not win her favor. All of us have received injustices in our lives. But lying down and making excuses for why we can't do anything to better our lot is antithetical to the path of Artemis. I believe that those who raise themselves up and make a rewarding life for themselves in spite of being victimized most certainly earn her favor.

As a sister and daughter, her familial aspects are evident. Even a superficial understanding of the mythos reveals her adoration for her brother and father. She aided her mother in the birth of her brother and for that she is invoked during difficult childbirth. I can imagine that many an expectant father prayed to her to ease the pains of his beloved.

So how can a man honor her?

Treat people without gender or orientation bias. Even though Western Society has made advances, we're not there yet. Members of the LBGT communities are regularly the targets of brutes looking to take out their aggressions on those they label as different or weak. It doesn't necessarily take a heroic rescue to honor her in this respect. Take it a step further than not laughing at the gay-bashing jokes by making it clear that you won't tolerate it in your presence.

In regards to sex, a person's "no" should be respected. It doesn't matter if she was begging for it a moment ago, no is no. Offer someone assistance if it looks like they are being harassed with unwelcome advances. Yes, you'll need to be ready for a violent reaction, but it's no excuse for moral cowardice.

Be the protector of those around you, strangers or no, who cannot protect themselves. Most times this won't require punching anyone in the nose. It's my experience that voiced disapproval of boorish behavior is enough to scare off most. If that's not sufficient there's no shame, especially in our litigious society, in calling for help.

Set the example for other men. Appreciating the beauty of a particular person is fine, but not to the extent of embarrassing her. Know the difference between admiring and objectifying.

De-mystify a woman's cycle and reproductive processes. Who's the real man, the one who refuses to go to the pharmacy and buy feminine hygiene products for his beloved or the man that realizes that his partner is uncomfortable and is happy to have an opportunity to help? A caring man takes responsibility for his safe-sex and contraceptive needs instead of leaving it to his partner.

I suspect that the phrase "women's work" is among her least favorite in our language. I take pride that I can wash dishes, cook, change diapers, sew and a hundred other things that some people put in that category. Not just because you should share work with your partner, but having those skills makes you independent. Robert Heinlein once said:

"A human being should be able to change a diaper, plan an invasion, butcher a hog, conn a ship, design a building, write a sonnet, balance accounts, build a wall, set a bone, comfort the dying, take orders, give orders, cooperate, act alone, solve equations, analyze a new problem, pitch manure, program a computer, cook a tasty meal, fight efficiently, die gallantly. Specialization is for insects."

How many of those things can you do well? I would suggest that the process of learning any one of those would be a worthy offering to her. When you have children raise them to be "people" first. Gender should not restrict their participation in society.

Strive to be self-sufficient. The world does not owe you a cookie. The only thing it owes you is the eventual end of this existence.

Artemis

by Thista Minai

Lady, You Who hunt in the wood,
Run with the beasts of the forest,
You have done my spirit such good,
I cannot help but adore You.

String Your bow and ready Your steed,
Gather Your quiver and arrows.
You know Your target will bleed;
You honor it as You pursue it.

Lady fire Your bow;
Now my courage must show.
Come, come killing blow!
I desire to know.

Your feet are running through the woods
but it can't hear You coming;
How you manage that I'll never know.
Silent are you stalking;
there it stands unknowing
that its Lady's come to hunt it.
Suddenly it sees you.
There it goes! It's fleeing
and off after it You ride.
Quick, You're gaining on it!
Now You are upon it;
soon this creature fine will die.

Lady fire Your bow;
Now my courage must show.
Come, come killing blow!
I desire to know.

Moon on Earth, You bless my life.
How glad I am to know You.

A Tale of Two Gods

by Frater Eleuthereus

Two Sides of The Same Coin

I think the best way to describe the differences between the Goddesses Diana and Artemis are that they are similar Ladies, of the same coinage. They are not just equal correspondences. They are Sisters, Lunar Deities who share a love of the Hunt and helping the disenfranchised, they pursue their goals with vigor in unrelenting fashion. Both are patrons of women, the land, particularly the forests, its lush flora and fauna. They both are the rulers of its half-lit realms of moisture, vegetation, trails, streams – and the creatures of myth in those lands bow to them alone.

They are also both nearly twin evolutions of each other. Diana was already a hunter and warrior to the Aricians before the myths of Artemis were equated to the Roman's Diana of the Aventine. In fact, it was this Hill of the Aventine, one of the seven hills upon which Rome was founded that Diana's temple was built and dedicated during the Ides of August, the time of Trivia. Her statue was replicated after the Great Mother of Ephesus. And now, in our time, that Wonder of the Ancient World, the Temple Premiere of Diana and Artemis (the Artemision) at Ephesus is now being re-imagined and rebuilt.

Ponder the excitement of that!

But to get back to the stars of this anthology: who are these two Ladies and why do they always seem to be found in each other's company? Are they one and the same? They certainly are similar enough in certain ways, but absolutely not in a mechanical correspondence manner as many Wiccans or arm-chair myth readers would have us believe. In the talk of coins, one is heads to the other's tails: which is which I cannot say. But they are both made of the highest grade of silver known.

Wonder Woman as Diana Victrix in Modern Heroic Myth

If we can stretch our imagination and disbelief for a moment to think of where to find Deity in the modern world, it will help us to answer the root question of who Diana and Artemis are and why they are always together. One of the best ways to answer this is to analyze one of the most iconic modern treatments of myth through an examination of the heroes of our age, particularly one of Time Warner subsidiary DC Comics' most enduring icons, Wonder Woman.

To imagine the goddess Diana in human form, we have only to look at Wonder Woman. After all, Wonder Woman's alter-ego is even named Diana Price. Wonder Woman is an Amazon of amazing strength armed with invincible bracelets that deflect all attacks. She also has a razor sharp tiara, a sword and her famous lariat of truth. But it is not these weapons which make her the Peerless Amazon – rather it is her skill and discipline that allowed her to best all of her competitors to win her title.

Diana was raised in Paradise on an island inhabited only by women. She left her home to go out into a world of danger, potential, and uncertainty. That world is our world, the world of man. This is the Wonder Woman, a comic hero to be sure, but also a manifestation of that timeless archetype, Diana Victrix, the Diana of Victory at her finest. Ever since the 1800's the archetype of Diana Victrix, the lone woman who pursues truth and her goals to the exclusion of all else, has been with us in many literary forms and Wonder Woman is the apex of this archetype in our modern world.

This archetype began, however, in ancient Greece in the form of the mothering yet completely free goddess Artemis. Central to this archetype – whether modern or ancient – is the hunt and the call of the wild to explore unknown lands. But for the modern era Diana, Wonder Woman, the unconquered terrain is our high tech crime ridden world, with its advancements and possibility, the so-called patriarch's world.

Diana and Artemis as Ladies that Strike Out Against Stagnation

Diana Price, cleverly named after the Goddess of the Hunt and Personal Freedom, can never be contained. Boredom, is her archnemesis, her initiator and we can relate to this one and all. Think of it in this light; inaction can be the enemy of many of us. How many times have you called a friend and asked how they were and heard "same old same old." Inwardly, you breathed and there was an awkward pause. You wished for more, but didn't know how to seek it or how to attain it. Artemis and Diana are your Ladies to help with that new path.

Imagine being on an island with thousands of women where that "same old" was the case for years! That is how it was in the DC Comic myth, where the Amazons all live secluded on an island hidden in the folds of time and space, Themiscyra.

Imagine being a child on this island of idealized compulsive yet caring warriors. Many of us would yearn for a new thrill, a new challenge to redefine our reality and place in the universe. And so it was that when man crashes on this island, a contest is called for and a certain girl disguises herself and enters it against her mother's wishes to pursue her passion for freedom and to do what is right. And thus was born Wonder Woman.

The shadow side of the goddesses Artemis and Diana are that their freedom can yield unrelenting xenophobia and isolation. It is the child Diana who was not wronged by the struggles against men who breaks her sisters free of this isolation and brings with her the hopes and the ideals of her people to a new land in need. Like the Knights who sought to bring the Grail to the "Dying land," she brings with her the power of the Mysteries of Womankind and attempts to resolve the ancient with the modern. But to do this, she had to begin somewhere. She needs to pursue a goal and reach it. If she did not, the alternative would be stagnation or cultural death.

The Amazons, we established, needed a little chaos, they needed to come back to the world. Not so much as messiahs, but because men and women often work better together than apart. I do not mean this in an intimate sense but in the context of team work. Resolution of the War of the Sexes is core to Diana and Artemis. But their primary objective is to fulfill their yearning to explore that final frontier. For the ancients it was the boundless forests. But now that nature has been "confined" and we restrain ourselves in urban metropolises, the new frontier is the patriarch's world, its cities and industrial mazes. And so boredom and freedom from restraint is most certainly the impetus for getting Diana and her people off of their Amazonian keisters and exposed to a whole new world that is filled with poverty, aggression, selfishness, but also glamour, technology, children, humor, tenderness; in short a world of insatiable variety and endless enthusiasm.

What Amazon girl wouldn't want to explore every facet that this brave new world has to offer?!

Diana Victrix as Lunar Avatar and the Initiator and Balancer of Ares

Now Wonder Woman has gone through ups and downs as a character from her beginnings in the 1940s through to the 21st century and hopefully beyond. She has had some instances of great as well as poor writing, but in it all we can still see her as a re-imagined Goddess for the modern world. A central theme in her modern mythology is her relationship and in some senses Initiation by the adversarial god Ares and the conflicts that he introduces. Wonder Woman, sprung from the womb of Gaea, fights against an array of villains to help save our world from them – and often itself.

Indeed it is Ares who watches her fight the Gorgon Medousa in one modern story arc (*Wonder Woman* volume #2, #205-213), which culminated in a fight televised around the globe. The dark witch Circe, Diana's shadow self (a champion of the power of Hekate), plans to kill millions by using Medousa as a weapon and making the innocents watch the Gorgon's petrifying stare. In a desperate move, Diana decides to save the world by blinding herself. She endures the wounds of the Gorgon's serpent venom, and through her sacrifice is able to face her shadowy other half, ultimately beheading the monster and saving countless innocent lives.

Victory also comes to her in her ongoing quests by maintaining and improving her purity and by using her golden lasso, which was given to her by the Olympians themselves. When anyone is bound by this lasso, they are compelled to speak only the truth. As an interesting aside, Wonder Woman's creator William Moulton Marston invented the lie detector – an instance where Diana's powers transcend the comics page to cross over into our world.

Think for a moment about the symbolism of this Golden Lasso of Truth. Is it not the very coils of the Qaballah's golden Tiphareth, the Sphere of Truth and Beauty wrapping around Diana like a serpent giving her enlightenment and clarity – insight, *gnosis*, a direct connection to her Inner Light and the Realms of Binah and Kether?

And when the light of that Sun is glowing around her, Diana is at her best – darting past the potential energy of Yesod and climbing her way up the Qaballistic spheres to Binah and beyond. She does this by balancing her super powers with an unrelenting quest for inner truth and the refinement of her character. But it is her capacity for compassion, her kindness and love towards others – and herself – that allows her to wield the nearly limitless powers of a Goddess with Prudence and Temperance.

Diana is also a reflection of those she serves. She provides them hope, empowerment and gives them the compassion of a Goddess for their sins when the truth of the lasso lays their souls bare. Mercedes Lackey touches on this briefly in her Introduction to Gail Simone's Wonder Woman story arc *The Circle*. But it goes beyond this. Diana can peer into the souls of those she entwines with her lasso. When she fights, she fights with just enough force to win. She knows through training and discipline the precise amounts of force to wield. And so it is that Diana the Wonder Woman can be seen as a re-invention of one of the Highest Lunar and Female Avatars of the Roman Diana portrayed in modern fiction. So she becomes the Pillar of Mercy for the DC Universe and modern heroic myth.

It is also with that very special lariat that Diana provides the power of truth which allows Ares to discover an important insight. If unchecked by the Pillar of Mercy's avatar, Diana, Ares will unleash a plague of war which could destroy the world. (This was shown in a seminal story arc by George Perez in the late 1980s, collected as Wonder Woman trade paperback *Gods and Mortals*.) This represented an important change in the character. Before the 1980's we often saw Wonder Woman with bouncing curls and a big smile, or trapped in some improbable bondage scene. But with this arc, the character of Diana was re-imagined as a hearty Greek Amazon with dialogue that would ring true for many a Hellenic Reconstructionist.

In that tale Lord Ares, embodiment of all that is War, the Dark and Noble sides of Man, his capacity for Protection but also unbridled Destruction, challenges Diana to teach man to overcome their base flaws. He in essence challenges Diana to fight the Shadow of Man and Himself, to prove to Him and the world that the man's world can have hope and be more heroic. And so we see the confrontation of the Ideal Man and the Ideal Woman, the Pillar of Severity and the Pillar of Mercy, providing a challenge for improvement and the redemption of the Dying World, which brings about the Middle Path of Balance.

And isn't that what any spiritual path is all about in the end, beauty and truth and balancing force with love? The Gods can be a great help in this, as their Initiation leads us into the Better, and they help us to improve ourselves and the world through the acquisition of *arête*, excellence or virtue. In a way, this can be equated to the Ephesian holy word or letters which lie at the heart of the mysteries Artemis of Ephesus, the Great Mother Goddess: AISION. It is not a meaningless word as some authors would have you believe. Rather, it is a core Ephesian concept that brings us back to self-improvement through mastery of mind, body, character and action.

Artemis and Diana

In the mid-1990's Diana came to a point in her comic where her mother Hippolyta called for her to be replaced. In a story that had far reaching consequences, *Wonder Woman: The Contest*, and *Wonder Woman: The Challenge of Artemis*, Diana's soon to be compatriot in arms and her greatest friend and competitor in the modern era of comics is a mysterious Amazon of Middle Eastern descent named of all things, Artemis. And in a story that was a contest to replace Diana the Wonder Woman, who better than an unknown named Artemis to take on that mantle?

Who is this re-telling of our Unbowed Lady, this Artemis? As written by the author William Messner-Loebs, she hails from the City of Women (Bana-Mighdall) is lithe, taller than our raven haired Diana and wears very little clothing. She cannot fly and while her strength is only Olympic human, she is Diana's match and more.

In her first few scenes she out-skilled Diana with the use of a bow and shoots an arrow through Diana's arrow into the center of a target. Recalling that our comic book Diana has great strength, incredible speed and the power of flight (that invisible jet is just for passengers these days for those that need an update) this isn't something to scoff at. Thus it is even more important when considering Artemis' victories later in the stories.

During a contest in which she bests every Amazon, Artemis becomes for a time, The Wonder Woman. Artemis overcomes her mightier sister, her flip side through hard work and persistence. And to top it all off, she even manages to save Diana. This shows a lesson that is a root for both the mythic and graphic novel versions of these Deities. Might doesn't always make right, even for an Amazon lady! For her victory over Diana, her Other, she is granted the Gauntlets of Atlas that magnify her strength and Hermes' Sandals, after which she is shown darting through the air she and gliding on the winds, all the while smiling like a child.

Artemis' time as Wonder Woman can be found in the trade paperbacks I referenced and they share many links both hidden and apparent in these stories. They are terrific modern tales of heroism and I would not wish to ruin all their plot points in this essay. But I would be amiss if I didn't hope this paper helps inspire a few people to go and read up on these Amazing Amazons.

Many readers of this anthology may well be wondering, "Where is all this going? How is Artemis or Diana, these modern Wonder Women, of relevance to us?" "We want academia," you might be shouting. "Give us the meaty stuff on the Lunar Ladies!" Ah, that would be missing the entire point. For Olympianists, this probably sounds familiar and you are hopefully pausing and raising an eyebrow in recognition by now.

Artemis as a human character climbs up skyscrapers with ease, a puff of red hair flickering in the distance as she is seen (barely) from one place to the next. Wielding with ease either an impossibly large sword or bow and arrow, she stands as peer and equal to her insanely powerful sister. Her choices and desire to help the world result in ominous circumstances as well. Her tale is one of gifts bequeathed to her by Gods, betrayal, love and sacrifice. In essence the core of the myth of a Goddess that limits Herself to a Human form and sacrifices Herself so that Her Other, Diana can save the world.

Diana of the DC Comics then goes to the Afterlife – Hades/Hell – and back to save Artemis her sister, her other, in order to bring her back to life in a mini-series called *Artemis Requiem*. This could have easily been a re-telling of the initiations at Aricia where our Goddess Diana saves Virbius during the three day festival of Trivia during the Ides of August. Which is paralleled by the story where Artemis goes to Hades to find Hippolytus and resurrects him as her Rex Nemorensis, thus showing a continuity through Greek, Roman, and modern mythologies.

And so we find that these Goddesses have not died, as so many Christians would have us believe; rather they are found as recurring co-existing symbiotic archetypes. They are very much breathing, lush, alive and hunting in modern stories and still altogether noble and inspirational. They are there to teach us the value of life, the weight of death and help its vulnerable or voiceless ones to rise and become something more by being beacons of hope and the makers of Heroines and Heroes.

Prayer for Artemis

by Melia Suez

I honor you Artemis:
Friend, Lover, Sister, Mother, Mistress.
Faultless,
You stand at my side despite my faults.
Freedom,
help me to love where I will.
Movement,
Teach me to run, dance and laugh.
Nurturing,
Aid me in raising my son.
Independent,
Guide me to be strong, whole and proud.
Friend, Lover, Sister, Mother, Mistress.
I honor you Artemis.

Hymn to Artemis of the Poisoned Earth

by Rebecca Buchanan

Hail Artemis
Lady of Strip-Mined Mountains
Lady of Denuded Forests
Lady of Back-Filled Swamps and Drained Marshes
Hail Artemis
Lady of Dying Wilderness

Artemis Alpheia

by Scott B. Wilson

The Bull of the River
Circled and splashed
His nostrils open wide
Seeking out the scent
Of Leto's fair daughter

He could taste the mud
And the moss
And the fish
And the birds
But not what he desired most

Far-Shooter, Wearer of Hides
Stood motionless on the bank
Like the quails she had dispatched
As a young girl in the mountains
With her first golden arrows

Alpheios could taste the mud
And the moss
And the fish
And the birds
But not what he desired most

Easer of Childbirth, Tender of the Young
Stood quiet with the wet white clay
Slowly drying as Helios climbed higher
Cracking at her lips, her armpits, and
The place that Alpheios most desired

Fish-tailed King could taste the mud
And the moss

And the fish
And the birds
But not what he desired most

Killer of Niobe's Children, Defender of Mothers
Knew she must soon make a move
Before the River God discovered her
Quiver and bow lay just in reach…
But, then, a branch snapped!

Alpheios turned his head
No animal was this
Not a deer
Not a boar
But what he desired most

Arethusa had walked all morning
Eager to bathe with Artemis
And her retinue of nymphs
She was young and pure
But not ready to wed

Alpheios moved closer to the sound
The pale flesh, the wide eyes
Long black hair falling to her waist
Overwhelmed by his passions
He thought this was the Goddess herself

Hooves turned to calloused hands
That grasped Arethusa's thin wrists
As he knocked her to the ground
With a sweep of his spiny fins
Finally, he would have the Goddess herself!

Daughter of Thundering Zeus, Sister of Just Apollon
Would not allow this girl to be sacrificed
As River God's tongue pushed into Arethusa's mouth
He tasted only the pure water of a spring
Which then flowed into the river currents

The Bull of the River
Circled and splashed
His nostrils open wide
Seeking out the scent
Of the maid Arethusa

He followed her to the sea
Around islands
Around rocks
Around ships
Until he reached Sikelia

Lady of Quails, Bringer of Light,
Split open the hard salty ground
And allowed fresh water to bubble up
Becoming her sacred home
Inviolate

The Bull of the Sea
Circled and splashed
His nostrils open wide
Seeking out the scent
Of the maid Arethusa

Alpheios climbed onto the Ortygian shore
Fishermen thought he was Poseidon
And feared earthquakes would follow
What had they done to anger him?
But the Bull soon left

White One, Saviour
Returned to the River
Without a God
And the nymphs greeted her as
Alpheia

Artemis and Lykastos

by P. Sufenas Virius Lupus

The days of hunting, of forest chasing
for Phylonome came to a close
the humid afternoon that the shepherd
approached, enticed, and seduced her.

Artemis, ever-vigilant virgin
smelled the seed the shepherd left.
No mortal seed was it, sulfurous
and ferrous its rusty aroma.

Ares had ravished the daughter of Nyktimos,
now forever cast out from the troop
of maidens accompanying the Lady
of Far-Shooting and Firebrands.

In anguish and distress Phylonome birthed
twins alone, no goddess or good woman
present as midwife; in fear of her father,
she cast them into the Erymanthos.

A noble she-wolf – strange the tale –
dropped her own pups by the scruffs
of their necks into the rushing river
to make room for the helpless humans.

No barks nor howls upset the night
when the two infants sucked
at the teats of the wolf-bitch
in the hollow of the oak tree.

They would have become hunters,
stalkers of prey in packs

had not another shepherd
taken in the stray children.

Gyliphos, turning the feral boys
from wild men to watchmen
tamed them, clothed them,
called them by their names:

Parrhasios and Lykastos, brothers
of Arcadian lineage. No sheep
was taken by wolf nor dog, thief,
bear, nor mountain lion under their watch,

but no neighbor's flocks were free
of depredation, true sons of Hermes
as the boys were, stealing, raiding,
taking their increase of wealth.

Helios in his heights one summer,
sweltering the sky under Sirius,
looked down at Lykastos lounging
in the shade of a leaf-crowned laurel.

Parrhasios tended the flocks far away
while Lykastos ventured forth seeking
the spoils of neighboring herds or hunts.
He laid his pedum and chlamys aside,

the sweat glistening on his fair form
yearning to cool in the clear breeze
but denied in the downpour of heat,
his resting breaths heaving in his lungs.

It was then he heard the sound--
a splash like chimes on the wind,
the silvery singing of water
playing upon living flesh.

Thinking not of anything
but to see what could make
a sound so sweet and vibrant
he rose from his rest and started

into the dark thickets and paths
overgrown with weeds and brush.
Nettles stung his naked skin,
thorns and sharp sticks scratched

and bled him, but he paid little mind
to the minor irritations.
The sound sang its chorus still,
and he found upon the whispered breeze

a scent like silver pine boughs.
He came to a clearing, showered
in rays of sunlight streaming forth
upon the waters of a forest pool.

Among the water lilies was a whiteness
of uncovered flesh that paled
the flowers' color completely:
Artemis of pristine splendor.

Lykastos' eyes drank in the sight –
the pool, the lilies, the Lady, the light,
the silver speckles of splashing water –
with holy awe and utter calm.

The cooling bathing activity forgotten,
the divine maiden stared in silence
at the amazed youth before her.
She saw his firm flesh, and asked,

"What is it that you want?"
His throat dry, his head parched,
the words like sand through his gullet,
"Only a drink of water."

She marveled at the naked man,
his beautiful penis hanging slack,
thinking back to Aktaion's intrusion
and his unrestrained erectness.

"Only water? Then approach, boy!"
Her heart jumped within her breast...
What was this? Restraint, humility,
fearlessness...had slain her?

He stood at water's edge, eyes downcast,
bending, kneeling, cupping his hands
for a sip of the cool spring's drink.
His ivory flesh was so close to hers...

But surely he was imperfect, prone
to lust and hubris like all men?
No, like any animal of the woods
his mind was on the water alone.

With a flash of her hands a flail
appeared; she brandished it high,
water drops cascading from its tails,
bring it down harshly upon

the back of Lykastos, intending
to tempt him, teach him, turn him
into the raging beast she thought, knew,
lurked inside his feeble flesh.

He lapped at the water, quivered
under the unexpected blow,
faltered, spilled the liquid
from his surprised fingers.

Again, never looking up,
he cupped his hands and drank,
sipping the sweet water

to quench his summer thirst.

Confused, insulted, Artemis asked,
"Anything else you want, boy?"
Between laps, breathing heavily,
Lykastos made an answer,

"Perhaps to hunt successfully later,
only if it is your will that I do."
The goddess laughed at this –
amazed, impressed, enamored.

"It is at my side you shall do so!
Be in the form of a wolf
and have the senses of a wolf,
but the reason of a human, now!"

Where once there was skin, fur
covered Lykastos' muscles, his
two arms now two legs, his face
a muzzle, his ears high and pricked,

a tail from his back side wagged,
his eyes golden and keen.
For a day and a night
under sun and moon they chased

every deer from its thicket,
every hare from its burrow,
fowl from trees and frogs from ponds,
and even mosquitoes in the night air –

but not one beast was felled,
not a drop of blood spilled,
no arrows flown to their marks
or snares set found their victims.

And when the chase was done,
wolf and woman rolled around

on the edge of the pool where they met,
playfully with aroused blood boiling

but never coupling all the while.
Lykastos slowly regained his shape,
clinging tightly to Artemis' side,
his skin still covered in fur,

his head still lupine lying
on the shoulder of the lady,
his sharp-nailed hand clutching
beneath the breast of the resting goddess.

She placed her hand on his head:
"May you always have the strength
and ferocity of a rabid wolf,
but the sense to use it wisely."

His toothed maw gleamed as cheeks
pulled back in a canid smile.
She put one hand on his groin
and spoke a further blessing:

"May the seed within you
be the roots of a mighty race
of heroes, of hunters, of wise men
who know not of Aktaion's fault."

Lykastos awoke beneath the laurel,
the sun still beating down around him.
With the back of his hand he wiped away
beads of sweat from his forehead.

In the distance he saw approaching
bright Chryses and lovely Cyparissos.
Lykastos laid back and smiled,
aroused, looking down at himself.

Prayer to Artemis

by Astalon

Hail to you Artemis, Maiden of the Forest, Lady of the Hunt, she who is wreathed in the moonlight. Greetings to you Dancer in the Night, Lady of the Living Waters, Shield to the Weak, Bane to the Oppressor.

How little do people know of you Divine Virgin. You are the Strong One who strives for the furthest reach, who scales the unassailable peaks, who roams in the forest deep. Where men sigh thinking they have reached their limit you show them that much more is left to explore, to discover, to achieve. When men stagger and quit you extend your hand and hold theirs, urging them to go on. When men balk and halt you dare them to continue, to break through their barriers.

How little do people know of you Pure One. You are the Merciful One who cradles the smallest and weakest of creatures in your arm, calming them with your sweet voice and shielding them from harm. You are the Helpful One who help all being grow strong and roam the beautiful body of Gaia. You are the Lovely One who teaches all beings of the wonders and beauty inherent within Nature, for you share your love of Gaia with all living beings. However you too are the Fierce One who with your mighty rifle lay low the fiercest and most baneful of beasts. You are the Accurate One whom no beast can dodge the bullet of your unerring aim. You are the Forest Flame that consumes and flattens the mighty woodland so that new life and new trees may regenerate.

How little do people know of you Savior and Destroyer. You are the Healer who with a single smile rejuvenates and revitalizes the pious, the kind and the worthy. You too are the One who with a single frown withers and weakens the impious and the wicked.

You are the Supreme Midwife whose very presence hastens and make painless the passage of a child into the world. Every woman in labor would praise your name for they know in the absence of your deliverance all they will know is pain and anguish.

And thus Blessed One do we honor you!

The Death of Actaeon

by Jennifer Lawrence

He runs,
The hounds at his heels,
Head heavy with horn,
Heart heaving.

Silver light filters down through green,
Lunar radiance bleeding through
Branches of birch and beech;
He can hear their belling and baying,
See the flashing fangs.

Close, so close, too close –

Panting, he stumbles,
Panting, he falls.

In a flash, they have found him.
Teeth tearing, snarling and snapping.
Scarlet, splattered –
Meat, muscle, blood spilling over the softly-crumbling moss.

He can see her with his dying eyes,
One hand that is a hoof raised
In agony, entreating –
Her eyes hard and cold as she turns away –
Hard, cold, and as bright as her light.

O Artemis! Cruel, proud, merciless!
What man ever suffered such transfiguration?
What child born ever grew to such rebirth?

Yet he can still recall the trembling moment that he saw her at the
    spring –
Nude, gleaming, clad in moonlight and dew,
Kneeling to wash in those chill waters,
Eyes flashing in fury
As his favorite hound betrayed him with a hunter's growl.

The deer's last moan fades –
Beautiful.
So beautiful.
That stolen glance, her naked form –
Death was worth it.

Healing with Artemis

by Amanda Sioux Blake

It was Athena, forever and always my first love, my first God, who introduced me to Artemis of the Wilds. I was perhaps fourteen years of age, and awkwardly aware of my body changing with the onset of puberty. I was intensely uncomfortable with the gawking stares of both the boys in my classes and men many years my seniors. My own sexuality was beginning to emerge, always a terrifying experience for a young girl. My feelings on this subject were already complicated, to say the least, thanks to my puritanical upbringing, and further muddled by an attempted sexual assault.

I was already awash in teenage angst, distressed by the never-ending custody battle following my parents' divorce, confused and frightened by the unforgiving jungles of middle school. When I made a foolish attempt to run away from home, my already fragile psyche was thrust into another maelstrom of emotions. The truck driver who picked me up alongside the highway and drove me far from home tried to force himself on me. I was one of the lucky ones – I got away before anything could happen. But the shock and the violence of that episode stayed with me. When I returned home that evening after calling my father amid sobs from the rest stop, I was further bullied by a local cop who took it as his duty to lecture me on the dangers of the wide world "out there." Despite my trauma, I resented being talked down to like that. Headstrong as always, I refused to validate his arrogance by reporting what had transpired.

I remained silent for years, my anger and resentment festering in the dark. I became extremely distrustful of the male gender. I dressed in men's clothes, the biggest and baggiest I could find, to hide my developing curves. When well-meaning girls at school tried to hook me up boys, I loudly declared that I was asexual and was going to remain a virgin till the day I died.

And it was to this chaotic mess that Artemis arrived. She was wild and fierce and free and intensely protective. She was primal Woman, whom no man can touch. She was exactly what I needed. She drew me into a safe, woman-centered womb, where I could heal from the trauma inflicted on me. With women Artemis is soft and motherly, tender and gentle and understanding. Even in myth, this fierce Virgin Goddess heard the pained cries of women in childbirth and hastened to their birthing beds to ease the pains of women she ordinarily would not have had much contact with. But let any man try to violate that sacred circle, and this nurturing Goddess would become the fierce, hard-hearted protector of virginity and innocence that Aktaion encountered. At the same time She nurtured me, She gave me permission to rage, to scream, to cry.

But like my ancient Greek sisters, I could not stay in the realm of Artemis forever. In Athens, when girls were married they left their childhood toys and dolls, along with locks of their hair, on the altar of Artemis. Artemis, protectress of the young. And so they passed from her sphere to Hera's.

Despite my loud protestations in my teenage years, I did eventually meet a good, decent man who set my heart on fire. Artemis's presence in my life has since shrunk to a background one. Although I am somewhat saddened by this, I know that She has accomplished what She set out to do. She took an angry and damaged young girl under her wing, healed her wounds, and ushered her into the world, a strong, independent adult woman.

Touched by Artemis

by Barbara Artemis Rachel

Let's see. Greek goddesses...Athena: founder of Athens. Uh... Diana: goddess of the moon. Venus: goddess of love. What does this all mean anyway?

This was me twenty years ago. That is, until I did a group that a therapist was giving on the Greek goddesses and how their stories impact women's lives. It was a group that was initially to be 12 weeks long and extended itself to two years: two hands-on, experiential, ritual-filled years.

At the end of it, I knew the difference between the Greek goddesses and the Romans, I saw how they were inherently intertwined in the natural world, and that there was one strong goddess that I was drawn to above all the rest: Artemis, who was so much more than just the goddess of the moon.

As I began to write this, I was thinking over the ways Artemis has been a part of my adult life. But I am now pulled up short by the scene portrayed in a black and white photo I have framed on my bookcase. It is me at 14 years old standing next to my 11 year old brother. We are standing with hands joined and homemade bows raised aloft in triumph in our other hands. This captures the passion of our lives which was hours and days spent roaming the woods surrounding our neighborhood. Here we made up stories and became the heroes in them.

Central to our tales was the bow and arrow. We were constantly in the throes of making them or shooting them. It never occurred to us to ask for a store-bought bow. We simply found just the right flexible branch and through experimentation strung it tight enough to project our carefully made arrows at least two or three feet in front of us. Our imaginations provided the rest of the distance.

These years spent alone in the woods with no adult supervision were safe and serene and shaped both of our lives to come. I know that Artemis was there as our protector even then.

Much later on, I received another sign which I did not recognize until I learned who Artemis is. In the basement of our first house the former owners had left a few items that were too big to bother hauling out at the time. One was an old wooden bureau with one stuck drawer. Nothing of interest. It remained slowly gathering mold until the day we decided to refinish the basement. Time to throw out this useless thing. However, one last look at the empty drawers. That day the stuck drawer sprang open when I tugged. For a moment I didn't know what I was looking at. Then I lifted out a beautifully made leather quiver, not a speck of mold on it.

I knew what I had to do. I called my brother, and through his connections found a classic recurve bow and some arrows to go with my quiver. For a long time I used this bow to shoot at a target set up next to the tipi I was moved to build and do ritual in. Hours and days spent in the woods, even in adulthood.

The image of Artemis as independent woman, free in her short tunic and safe in her knowledge and love of nature was the most compelling aspect of my patron for me. But her traits that tended to women in childbirth and by implication to a sisterhood of women independent of men was the next aspect to affect my life. It was when I finally revealed to myself and others that I was a woman-loving woman that I took Artemis as my middle name. Thus my whole name became a conscious symbol of the person I had transformed into: Barbara (my given name, connected to my heritage and reclaimed through its pagan meaning) Artemis (my patron and protector) Rachel (the name of my spirit guide who sits quietly by my side at the edge of the shining moonlit lake).

My day to day relationship with Artemis is one of familiarity and faith. She is the one I invoke while driving on a dark road in the country. "Artemis, please protect your animals from my car and protect me from harm." She is the one I smile to when I hear a rustle in the leaves by the path in the forest. She is my strength when listening to women tell me of their pain and abuse. She is me and I am her, Artemis, goddess of the moon.

Choices

by Allyson Szabo

Kayla brushed her dark, lustrous hair and carefully applied make-up to her pale skin. She looked at herself in the bathroom mirror, critical of her own appearance. She knew she was pretty, but today was special. Today, she was going to meet with Sean, her boyfriend of the past two months. Today, she was going to give herself to him.

She knew that sounded somewhat melodramatic, but she wanted it to be special. She was still a virgin, and had taken a whole week to make the decision that Sean was the boy she wanted to remember as "her first." She was excited and nervous, happy and unsure, all at the same time. Her tight jeans offset her lithe form, and when Sean looked, he would see the curve of her thong at the waistband of the low-rise jeans. Her mother would have a fit, but who cared? Mother was always having a fit about something. She was such an old lady at times!

After patting down her shirt, assuring herself that she looked fine, she skipped out the back door, backpack flung carelessly over one shoulder. She was going to meet Sean at school, and after classes were over, they were going back to his place. His parents were away on a business trip, and he had the whole house to himself!

***

Kayla was 14 years old, but was curved like an older girl. Alexandra, her mother, spent many sleepless nights worrying about her daughter's attractiveness to boys. She was worried Kayla would, like herself, get sucked into having sex too early. But she also knew that it was too hypocritical to punish her daughter for making the same choices that she had made as a teenager. How could she impress on Kayla that early sex meant losing your childhood, and taking on the mantle of adulthood much too soon?

Alexandra knew there wasn't much she could do, herself. She had instilled Kayla with as much knowledge and self-assurance as she could, and provided safeguards in as many ways as she was able. The rest was up to Kayla... and she still didn't trust her daughter. Kayla was headstrong and full of the fires of life and love, much as Alexandra had been in her youth. Kayla hadn't done anything wrong, though, so there was no reason to ground her or keep her around the house, or otherwise restrict her activities. That would be unfair, and wrong.

Alexandra turned to her altar, not sure what else to do. Her eyes lingered on the small statue of Artemis, the Virgin Huntress, near the back. Originally, she had worshiped Artemis almost exclusively, but as she had grown as a parent and as a person, Artemis had gently faded into the background. Now, she pulled the statue forward, and ran her fingers lovingly over the marble curves, caressing the tiny white face that was so similar to her daughter's. She wondered whether Artemis might not be the answer to her prayers...

***

Kayla sailed through school. Because Sean was older than she, they did not share any classes, but she saw him in the hallway from time to time between periods. He would wink and grin at her, and look her up and down, and she would blush and giggle and scurry off to her next class. Her whole being tingled, knowing that tonight, they would be as close as any two people could be! She watched the clock, waiting impatiently for the last bell to ring so she could rush off to meet Sean at the bus stop.

With only minutes to go, she tapped her manicured nails on the desk top, only half listening to Mrs. Smythe nattering on about the Civil War. She made note of the homework and when it was due, and was in the process of tucking her notebook into her backpack when the teacher approached.

"Kayla, I need you to do something for me tonight," Mrs. Smythe began.

Inwardly, Kayla groaned. Generally, she liked History and this teacher, but today she just wanted to be gone from here! "We have a new student, Diane, and she needs a bit of help with her homework. At her last school, they were covering another historical period, and she's behind a few weeks."

Kayla looked stricken, wanting to be helpful but also wanting to escape this unsought duty. "Mrs. Smythe, I really ..." Her voice trailed off as the new girl stepped out from behind the teacher. She found her mouth forming words she had not meant to say. "I really would be happy to help Diane." Why had she said that? Oh no!

Diane smiled silently, watching the interaction. She looked about 14, the same age as Kayla, but her eyes and facial expressions made her seem much older. She stood about five feet tall, considerably shorter than Kayla's 5'4", and her head was topped with dark, tightly curled hair. Kayla thought she was pretty, although her face was much rounder and her eyebrows much darker than the other girls she knew. Diane was also a bit – and Kayla noticed it without saying anything out loud – chunkier than the average girls in the school. Her hips flared out in a very feminine curve, and her legs and arms were well muscled and tanned. Her white dress was quite different, although not out of place. Kayla nodded to her, unable to find her voice again, after it had betrayed her... and Sean.

"Thank you, Kayla. Here is what I would like you to go over tonight. I appreciate your help!" Mrs. Smythe waved to the two girls and scuttled out of the classroom with Kayla's dismayed eyes following her.

"Hi," came a husky voice. "I'm sorry you have to help me, but I don't want to be too far behind." Diane shrugged and smiled again, and shouldered her book bag. "Why don't we go to my place to study?"

"Sure," Kayla muttered, trying not to sound upset. "But I need to let my boyfriend know I'm not catching the bus with him."

Sean was upset, giving Kayla that unconcerned guy shrug that said he wasn't as committed to her as she would like. He stuck his hands deep in his pockets and told her he'd see her tomorrow... maybe. With tears in her eyes, she turned back to Diane, and trudged along.

"I'm sorry I interrupted. Did you two have plans?" Diane's dark eyes scanned over Kayla's hunched body and damp eyes.

"Yeah, but whatever. I don't mind helping most of the time. Nice to meet you."

The two girls chatted on the bus ride, discovering several things in common. Kayla's spirits rose somewhat, and in her mind she made a note to talk to Sean about picking a different day to tryst. Diane was very likeable, had the same love of anime, and knew every word that Rupert Grint spoke in the *Harry Potter* books and movies. When the bus stopped to let them out Kayla barely looked around, she was so involved in her conversation.

It wasn't until a few moments later that she realized Diane was leading her into what looked like a big park with lots of trees.

"Where are we going?" she asked, suddenly feeling hesitant.

"My home is in here. My family is a bit, well, different. We're not so into cities." She smiled and shrugged, and trekked off into the woods.

Kayla followed, more intrigued than scared. "Is your family home?" she asked.

"Nah. My dad works out of town most of the time, and my mom has a lot of volunteer duties to take care of. Mostly I take care of myself. I have a brother, but he's always busy and I don't see him very often."

Diane picked a beautiful tree to sit under, and pulled out her history books.

The girls pored over the textbook, reading about General Grant and President Lincoln, proclamations and treaties, losses and victories.

When Kayla felt Diane was mostly caught up, the books disappeared back into their backpacks, and they resumed chattering about mutual interests. The one interest they didn't share, Kayla found, was boys.

Diane crinkled up her nose, and looked at Kayla from under her dark lashes. "Why would you want to mess around with boys?" she asked, a tone of distaste in her voice.

"Well," Kayla considered, "I like Sean. He's cute. He looks really nice without his shirt on..." Her voice trailed off, and she thought hard about the question her peer had just posed to her. Why *did* she want to mess around with Sean? Diane waited with sainted patience as the thoughts filtered through Kayla's brain. "I really don't know. I was... I was going to have sex with Sean today. But, in a way, I guess I'm kind of glad I'm here instead. Even though I was a bit resentful at first."

"I thought so, just by the way you looked when he walked off. But at this stage, aren't boys just big bundles of uncontrolled hormones?"

She laughed, a merry sound akin to fairy bells. "There's plenty of time to be grown up. You have the rest of your life to do it! Me, I'm free!" She stood up, and began to dance in circles around the tree they had studied under.

Kayla watched this free soul with fascination. "Don't you like to look at boys?" She was having a hard time conceiving of a person who didn't think of boys at least sometimes.

"Sure I do. I like to look at them, same as you. But that doesn't mean I have to drop my knickers for them!" Diane giggled, and blushed a bit. "They may not know it, and I guess most girls don't know it, but really, once you have sex with a boy, he kind of owns you. I mean, not like the Civil War women were owned by their husbands or anything," she rushed to explain, "But 'cause we're so young. We can't tell anyone but each other, and if we do tell, everyone thinks we're a slut. If we hide it, it's just a nasty secret that festers inside. But for the guy, it's like a badge of honor, and he gets points for it. No one thinks he's a slut, after all. We females just have nothing to gain from it," she concluded, and having finished her dance, she dropped down to the grass again to stare intently at Kayla.

"Wow. I... I guess I never thought of it that way before. Heck, I'm not sure I think of it that way now!" Kayla's head reeled from all the stuff Diane had just said. It made so much sense when she was saying it, but her hormones were telling her different things. She felt confused.

"Can I tell you about this group I belong to?" Diane looked intense and hopeful. Kayla nodded hesitantly, and Diane broke into another of her bright smiles. "It's called The Hunters of Artemis and it's a group of girls. We talk online. It's sort of like girl scouts, except it's on the computer, and there's members all over the world! You get to be a member until you have sex for the first time, then you have to leave. It's not that they shun you or anything, it's just... this is just for girls, and once you've had sex, you're not a girl anymore, and so you have to leave. But they give you a cool send-off and a party online and everything. My mom is really into it, and she thinks it's a great thing."

Kayla blinked. An online group for virgins sounded rather boring. She said as much. "How interesting can it be? A bunch of virgins?" She sounded more critical than she meant, but her mind was having difficulty wrapping itself around Diane's words.

"It's really interesting. We talk about boys sometimes, but not most of the time. We talk about school, and about jobs, and home life, and we share homework and proof read assignments for each other. We also learn hunter safety rules, and if our parents allow it, we learn how to use a bow and arrow. I'm really good at it," Diane puffed up a bit and looked very proud of herself. "My dad taught me how, and got me my bow and arrows. And I practice a lot. Do you want to try it out?"

***

Over the coming weeks and months, Alexandra noted a change in Kayla. She was a confused mother, as all mothers are when their children find a bit of self-control and maturity on their own, but she was a happy mother. Kayla became less boy-crazy, although she still dated Sean and talked about the Jonas brothers and other pop stars. She started helping out with some things around the house, offering to do dishes, and even cook a meal occasionally. At times, Alexandra wondered if the pod people had replaced her daughter with one of their own, but mostly, she just thanked her lucky stars. Kayla's grades went up a bit, and she asked to take up archery at school. Alexandra shook her head in awe, and took quiet notes on the Artemesian influences her daughter showed.

For her 15th birthday, Alexandra purchased a new statue of Artemis, and showed Kayla how to set up her own altar. They picked out a lovely leaf green altar cloth, and chose a vase for flowers, and a bowl for offerings. They even stitched together some tiny outfits for the statue to wear. Once a month, they would worship together, mother and daughter, sharing love, laughter and life.

Little Bears

by Rebecca Buchanan

they wore bear skins
those little girls at Brauron
stamped their feet and growled
growled from deep in their bellies
little girls don't dance as bears anymore
they throw up to stay weak and skinny
wear six inch heels that make them stumble and teeter
sculpt and paint their useless nails
hold their tongues and smile and don't growl
little girls aren't bears anymore

The Prayer of Kleia

by Sannion

I am Kleia, the daughter of Apollonia. My people are settlers from Khios and have lived here in Ptolemais for two generations now. We are Greeks, of a good family. My father is a tax-farmer, and my mother an assistant to the *kanephore* at the festival of the Great Goddess. But you probably knew that already, didn't you? You have been good to our family, helping my mother birth six children, four of whom survived.

I have come before you, Artemis, because I am to wed Demetrios, the merchant's son. I am told that he is very wealthy and frequently goes on important business up to the city for his father. My father says that he is a kind man, fond of books, and that he will provide well for me. I hope to give him many fine sons and to make him a happy man.

Before I am to wed him, though, I must put aside my childish things. And so I place here on your altar my ball and rattle, my comb and my favorite dress (the pretty one with the red stripe across the middle), and lastly this jointed doll, with the yarn hair that my mother made for me.

I call her Senni, because she reminds me of my Egyptian friend who had a big smile like my doll and would always laugh so hard when we played down by the river. The nymphs took her and I miss her. It is fitting, I suppose, that you should have this Senni too. I don't need her any more. She is a child's plaything and I am a woman now. I bleed and my breasts have started to come in. I should have given these things up long ago, but now I have no choice for I am to be Demetrios' wife.

It still sounds strange in my ears to say that. What do I know of keeping a house and raising babies? I never had an interest in such things, though all my girlfriends liked to pretend. It's all they talked about, in fact. I was much more interested in exploring down by the river, watching the crocodiles and the ibises feed on the fishes, and listening to the slave teach my brothers their Homer. I would sit beside them and daydream that I was one of your nymph companions, joining you in the hunt. Oh, to be so free and wild – how I loved those dreams! But all that is behind me now, isn't it?

These trinkets on your altar are the last ties to my childhood.

Care for them, would you?

They are important to me. Especially Senni. I loved her most of all.

I know I've already placed them there … but may I touch her, one last time?

And goddess? I know I shouldn't pray this. I am supposed to ask only for strong, handsome, brave sons, sons to make my husband proud. Give me those, please.

But could you also send me a daughter like Senni? The real Senni, not my doll. With a gentle soul, a big smile, and always laughing.

I think I would like that. I would brush her hair, and give her her own tutor to teach her Homer so that she didn't have to sneak her lessons, and I wouldn't force her to marry a boy she didn't know before she was ready.

That is my prayer, Artemis.

Thank you for listening to me.

I have to go now. The priest is waiting impatiently outside. I can hear his sandals on the flagstones as he restlessly paces back and forth.

Thank you again, from Kleia, who is going to be a good wife, you just wait and see.

To Bless a Child

by Frater Eleuthereus

Hear me in your dreams, child of the Hunter Moon.

I am the sacred pain and blood of womankind
That which brings the power of life and creation
I was the unseen midwife and guide,
Who helped your mother through the pangs of birth she
    endured alone,
To bring us you

Know Little One, you are loved and protected always by Diana,
    the Queen.

I am the maker of stars, worlds, and the galaxies of a
    billion names.
Feel my pride as you begin to crawl, walk and experience life.
The souls of heroes and champions spin around me.
They will inspire you to reach higher and higher
To be the best you can be

My skills, my beauty, my power are all yours to tap.

Fauns and nymphs will dance through your home and life.
They will make your eyes widen and sparkle in secret delights.
All manner of unicorns and faeries are yours to command.
I charge them all, to watch and care for you.
You alone will hear their pitter-patter on your rooftop and know
    its meaning.

I enchant your life with my warmth, freedom of spirit and love.

Remember my gifts as you grow older.
Never forget magick is everywhere.

Believe in the wonder of your heart.
Nurture the hero inside.
Help the world around you.

Sleep tenderly for Diana is here.
All this and more I give freely to you, my Tiny Light.
See me perched in the woods, and never fear.
I tense my mystic bow back,
Watching and waiting
Ready to smite evil and chaos that might never come
Welcome to the infant race and to my holy guard.

Artemis, Destroyer

by Allyson Szabo

Thou golden Artemis,
Incomparable beauty and inviolate virgin,
You of singing bow and perfect arrows,
Protectress of maidens and children,
I beg of you to hear my prayers.

Thou tall and stately goddess,
Reliever of the pangs of birth,
You also bring disease and death on swift wings.
Artemis called Prothyraia,
I beg of you to hear my prayers.

Thou destroyer of children,
Our unborn and sexless infant
Was struck by your unerring arrow,
Taken from us cruelly –
I beg of you to hear my prayers.

Thou terrible Maid,
You hold the right of life over the unborn.
You chose death for our babe,
And I can accept that, but...
I beg of you to hear my prayers.

Thou Artemis Paedotrophus,
Watch over our little one.
See that our child reaches Persephone's realm,
And is nurtured and loved as we would have.
I beg of you to hear my prayers.

Death and Dance

by Thista Minai

Wind sings on rocky cliffs,
rustles sunlit leaves,
plays the tune to which You dance
as hooves beat the rhythm of Your hunt.

Something startles, turns to flee.
Bow bends and arrows fly.
Dirt and sweat and blood mix;
voice cries, dust rises, doe falls.

Clear springs and mountain pools
welcome You to bathe.
With floral crowns and hunting calls
You dance the rest of Your day.

Artemis & Orion

by Kenn Payne

I only ever loved once; truly loved, as one would love the other half of their soul. It might be hard to imagine a chaste and independent Goddess such as myself admitting to such a thing, but I recall the events surrounding my feelings and my loss fresh in my heart and mind.

Ever since I had been young, sitting on my father's knee declaring my desires of independence, eternal virginity and a shining bow and arrows like my brother, advancing through womanhood to settle down, marry, and produce offspring of my own had never held interest.

The forests and mountains were my home, the creatures and nymphs my eternal companions. My life was blissful, free and full of frolic. I bathed in the crystalline springs and rivers on my travels, reveled with my entourage after a successful hunt; dancing to the sounds of lyre and pipes – lost in a happy abandon as I twirled and stamped my feet.

It was late one beautiful summer evening, when Helios' light shone bronze through the leaves, that I met him.

Strolling amidst the trees, relishing the coolness of the soft grass under my bare feet, I came across a clearing in the brush where a large black boar was foraging. I stood and watched it as it snuffled through the leaves and twigs. Then my eyes were drawn up to movement – ever so slight – in the cover of a large bush. The air displaced, a low whistling followed by a shrill squeal and the boar slumped on its side into the dirt and let out a single, rattling death sigh. Sticking out from its flank was a sturdy spear and as I continued to watch, the foliage parted and out stepped one of the most handsome men I have ever seen.

Standing several feet tall, he had short curls of chestnut hair and striking blue-grey eyes. His bronzed skin was smooth, the hairs on his exposed chest and arms somewhat bleached by exposure to the sun. He wore a simple cloth sash around his waist, held in place by a braided leather belt, a pair of dark leather sandals and across his back was a case which contained several half-length spears.

As he knelt at the side of the boar to remove his weapon, he suddenly glanced up and noticed me. I could not help but smile back at him when he nodded his head in greeting. His proficiency as a hunter had been fluid and flawless so as the boar had sensed nothing and felt little.

The irony was not lost on me that more than once before those foolish enough to look upon me met with certain grizzly fates, but as I gazed into those eyes I felt for the first time a stirring inside.

"Hello." His voice was strong and resonant. "I hope I did not startle you?"

I shook my head, a momentary lack of words at my command. "No, I am fine. What brings you here to Delos?"

"The hunting!" his face lit up in a broad smile as he took a knife from his belt in preparation of skinning his prey. "My name is Orion."

"Artemis."

"I know. My father told me about you."

"Your father?" My confusion was obviously apparent.

"Poseidon. Your uncle."

He didn't seem to take it personally when I explained I had never heard of him, but then my uncle, like my father, was known to have sired many offspring. I continued to stand watching him as he butchered his kill. We spoke about the beauty of Delos, his passion of hunting, his admiration of my abilities – all he had heard had come from surprisingly glowing recommendations from Poseidon himself.

From that first encounter I began to make my excuses to be in the forests and glades to hunt alongside him often. He was courteous and respectful and interested in all I had to say about hunting, ambushing, stringing a bow, throwing a spear. We laughed and often walked the sandy shorelines, watching Helios slip from the sky. At first we travelled with my following of nymphs and huntresses but soon I became strangely eager to spend time alone with Orion.

One evening as I returned to Olympos, I was met by Apollon at the gates. As usual he was immaculate; far removed from the soil and grass-stains of my khiton, the drying sweat on my brow and shoulders, strands of hair misplaced.

"Another long day?" he enquired as he began to walk with me.

"Yes, but worth it dear brother. I never tire of the chase."

"I hear from Nyrissa that you have not been hunting with her or many of the others lately."

I slowed and turned to look at him puzzled. "What are you getting at?"

"Nothing..." The pause that followed his word was soon filled again with his voice. "I just find it amusing that you would have asked Father for all those attendants only to push them to one side."

His tone was not one I liked and I stopped to regard him. "And where are the Muses?" I gestured around us with my arms wide.

"Having attendants does not make them slaves to us or vice versa. If I deem to take time by myself, I will do so!"

"Yes," he replied reflectively. "You've been taking a lot of time 'by yourself' lately."

"If you have something to say, brother, then come out and say it."

His amber eyes met my own grass-green orbs; his jaw was set hard and his expression authoritative and protective. "You've been hanging around with that giant, Orion."

"And...?" I was beginning to get impatient with his elusive and baiting statements.

"I suppose you did not hear about his previous escapades before he settled on Delos? The rape of a King's daughter on Khios and subsequent exile...?"

There was nothing I could reply. It was true I had been unaware of these things. But I found it hard to accept that Orion – my strong and handsome companion – could be capable of such violent actions. Obviously my face said as much as my silence as Apollon's expression softened as he held my face in his smooth hands.

"Sister, I want only for you to be safe."

Bitterly, I pulled away from him and walked on. "I can take care of myself."

I avoided Apollon after that – and Olympos in general. I spent my days in the woods with Orion and we hunted. We talked and laughed and what I felt I could not describe as much as I could not deny it. When, as we often did, we had watched Helios descend, I would take refuge in nearby caves and snuggle warmly with the she-bear who lived there.

Time passed and we grew closer, and although Apollon's accusations still rang in the back of my mind, Orion had been nothing but attentive and kind – strange for a man, I thought, mortal or otherwise. Together we brought down a graceful stag, whose thick hide made an excellent cloak for Orion. That same evening I found him squatting by a stream, obliviously working away on something unseen in his hands.

My approach did not startle him, yet he turned to look at me with some surprise. A moment later though and his face flushed with the smile that had long since come to warm my heart. He held out his hand and balanced on his palm was a small figure of a female archer carved out of the antler of the felled stag. I beheld its majesty; for although Orion was no artisan, the crude – but charming – figure captivated me with its primitive beauty.

He rose to his feet as I took his gift in silence. I looked at him and his eyes shone brightly in the twilight. For a moment I thought he might speak but silence hung between us.

I turned the figure over in my hands, feeling the smoothness of the whittled antler, tracing the simple striating patterns with my fingertips. We stood in blissful silence for moments after; Orion didn't seem to mind – it was obvious no words could express our truest feelings. Eventually we said goodnight and I retired to the bear's cave, clutching Orion's gift to my chest.

The next morning, after I had bathed in a cool spring, I found Apollon waiting for me at the entrance to the cave. At first I still felt the anger inside me from our previous encounter but seeing my brother after so long made me happy and I greeted him with a smile and an embrace. We talked little about what had happened previously and I was glad. At his suggestion we decided to walk the shoreline, telling stories of our latest escapades and Apollon filled me in on the latest happenings on Olympos.

"Hera and Father had another tiff three nights ago," he recalled with a bemused smile.

"Who about this time?" I replied knowingly.

"Some mortal princess; you know Father."

I did, and we shared the joke.

We soon returned to our usual selves and Apollon proposed a race. Eager to best my brother I accepted his challenge. He motioned to an outcrop of rocks just where the waves and foam lapped up at the sand and without a further word and only the slightest nod of his head, the race began!

My legs pumped hard, my bare feet hitting the soft, wet sand. I laughed as I began to inch away from Apollon, turning my head to smile and wave as I began to take the lead. A few minutes later and I stood atop the rocks, my hands on my waist, watching as Apollon reached the foot of the outcrop.

"You didn't even try!" I chided impishly.

"All that chasing deer has made you a formidable runner," he smiled back, catching his breath. "Let's see how your archery fares against mine."

The adrenaline of my athletic victory still fresh in my veins, to refuse such a challenge would have been foolish and met with Apollon's chiding remarks. So I took up my bow and smiled confidently at my brother.

"Whatever the target, my shot shall be swift and true."

If only I had realized what I was saying; if only I had more sense than pride, I might have been aware of Apollon's over-eager anticipation and the glint in his soulful, amber eyes.

He pointed out far across the ocean; to the furthest point on the horizon where – barely visible – a small, rounded shape could be seen bobbing up and down. My challenge was to hit it with a single arrow from where I stood.

Confidently, I notched an arrow in my bow and took aim. My eyes followed the length of the shaft and from the tip to where my target was situated, still bobbing on the horizon. With an almost inaudible sound, the arrow flew from my bow and whistled through the air towards its goal. In a matter of moments it had struck fast the mark and I turned immediately to Apollon with a beaming smile.

"I concede defeat, dear sister." He said with a courtly bow.

We continued our walk along the shoreline, oblivious to everything. It did not even enter my mind what it was that I might have been asked to shoot... a school of fish? Floating debris? A sandbank just peaking above the waves?

As the evening drew to a close, we returned back along the same stretch of beach. In the golden light of the setting sun, I saw a figure lying prone on the sands where the waters still lapped at their legs. A sense of urgency took hold of me and I increased my pace – if only slightly. Drawing closer to the form, I soon recognized my own arrow, artfully crafted, two-thirds of the shaft pointing skyward. The sand around the form was wet with sea water and stained dark with blood. A handful of steps closer and I paused in deep shock as I beheld the blank expression of the face staring back at me, grey-blue eyes glazed and empty.

The breath caught in my throat as I moved to be by his side but Apollon seized my wrist. Turning to him I could see an almost nauseated expression on his face. As Immortals we were often repulsed by death and the miasma that comes with it, but something inside me longed to be by his side.

"Leave him." Apollon said, simply.

I snatched back my hand, staring my brother dead in the eye. "You knew...you knew he was out there! You tricked me!"

"Artemis, he would have forced you to betray yourself! I acted out of my devotion to you and your safety. I had heard much about Orion that was distasteful; I was given consent by Zeus and Poseidon in this matter."

"And what about me!?" Tears were stinging my eyes. "You men with your arrogance and lording ways! Is it any wonder I forsake tying myself to the bridal bed and a life of obedience and appeasement!?"

"What's done is done."

His matter-of-fact tone cut me deep inside. I had known my brother to be callous – as had all the Gods. But he had never been so unkind to me before. I turned away from him as the tears began to roll freely down my cheeks. I took the last few steps to Orion's side and knelt beside him, cradling his lifeless form. My sobs of anguish were soothed little by the hushing of the sea and Helios slipped once more from the sky, staining the world with a blood-like illumination that spoke of Orion's demise.

Had I turned to regard my brother once more, I would have seen how deeply my actions had affected him at that moment. His eyes were lowered in shame and all accusation and righteousness had drained from his face. With the last glimmers of the evening sun, he vanished.

I spent too long to recall, cradling Orion to me. I rocked gently, my grief coming now in nothing more than tearless, noiseless sobs. I had closed his eyes and as I gazed into his face I could have been fooled into thinking that he was merely asleep.

It was at that moment I realized I was no longer alone. Glancing up, my eyes red-rimmed from my crying, I beheld Athena in all her glory. Standing graceful and tall, dressed in the simple white robes she wore on Olympos, her bronze-like curls tumbling down her back and across one shoulder. Her misty-grey eyes were soft as they regarded me and she knelt at my side and placed a hand on my cheek.

"Come sister, it is time for you to move on."

"I will not leave him to the crabs and the gulls!" My tears began to fall once again.

"Apollon has been beside himself with remorse over his actions." Athena said softly. "He petitioned our Father to have Orion brought back; he even went so far as to threaten to defy Zeus' will should he be refused."

"So..." My anticipation was short lived as I realized the look on Athena's face.

"Father will not break the base laws of the Cosmos, you know how highly He regards all matters regarding the Moirae. But in his shame, a compromise was garnered."

Athena's hand was soft but firm on my face and I leaned into it, closing my eyes against the swelling of grief I felt yet again. Hot tears trickled down from my eyes and Athena caught several in her hand. When she next opened it, nestled in the palm of her hand were three sparkling diamonds.

Silently, as I watched, Athena produced a needle and thread and proceeded to affix the diamonds to the belt Orion was wearing. When she had finished she looked at me kindly.

"He will last forever as we shall. His place is not in Olympos but he has a home in the heavens."

My heart was warm and my grief suddenly alleviated to a greater extent. I looked down once more at my peaceful, eternally slumbering hunter and slowly leaned to place my soft lips against his. The warmth of my love for him rushed through my body and into his and when next I opened my eyes, Orion was no longer the prone and lifeless form in my arms, but a cluster of crystalline fragments, pulsing with life and light.

Without a word, and with Athena at my side, I took up each piece; attached it to an arrow and let it fly into the bosom of Nyx. The Night Goddess received my love with open arms and to this day he can still be seen poised in the sky, my eternal hunter.

It was some time before I could truly forgive Apollon for his transgression, but to stay resentful for all eternity is a chore even for an immortal. Millennia after the incident, my brother gave me a splendid gift. He sent his Muse, Erato, to a mortal man named Alfred Lord Tennyson, inspiring him to write the crux of my tragedy:

I hold it true, whate'er befall;
I feel it, when I sorrow most;
'Tis better to have loved and lost
Than never to have loved at all.

Hippolytus, Beloved of Artemis

by Michael Routery

The strange figure of Hippolytus appears fleetingly in the secluded woods of Artemis/Diana in various classical texts, including the *Metamorphoses* and the *Aeneid*, but most prominently in Euripides' tragedy, *Hippolytus*. Hippolytus, called the "chaste hunter," is a devotee of Artemis, her mortal companion in the forest, the one male admitted to her inner circle, roaming in the woods with his own companions too. They are largely set off from the mundane civic world of the polis and particularly of the palace. Tellingly, Hippolytus was the child of an Amazon, the Queen Hippolyta, but his father was Theseus, King of Athens. His removal from the day-to-day world was particularly, one of removal from the intrigues and gossip of the girls and women of the palace. Euripides suggests this has alienated him from the goddess Aphrodite, and to have led to her unsettling of things; the play begins with the two goddesses standing at the gate of the palace. On the one hand Hippolytus is the noble youth, dedicated to his goddess Artemis, and to the wilderness life, on the other, he comes across as a sexist despiser of women, as when recoiling from the queen's desire, he castigates her entire sex, crying out to Zeus, "Better that men should come to your temples and put down a price, each what he could afford, — buy themselves children in embryo in gold or silver and get their money's worth; then they could live at home like free men without women!" (Euripides 46). He seethes with an intense intransigence, that hints of the non-human, a fierceness, an unyielding character that plays a large part in his undoing — and deification.

Apparently in Euripides' first version of the play, Hippolytus was a true tragic hero (Vellacott 18); however, when the playwright rewrote it in the version that we know today, it no longer fully fit the tragic model as there is no one clear tragic hero. Phaedra to some extent is the tragic heroine, but Theseus also, the tragic being distributed in this play. Hippolytus is just too non-human; he comes across as n queerly aloof figure. Everything about this chaste hunter is odd, even his origins bespeak a hybridism: his father, the king of Athens, his mother an Amazonian queen, a barbarian tribeswoman of the wild steppes beyond the borders of Greek order. But particularly, a strong feminine and otherworldly marking is stamped upon him, the "noble hearted one," as he is repeatedly referred to in the play. There is something feminine in his nature, as he remains virginal in his relations with human women. He does have a band of male companions, youths like himself who prefer their own company in the deep woods. There's seems a hint of the *männerbünde* bands, those outsider bands found in many archaic Indo-European traditions, such as the *fianna* of Ireland, that live in the borderlands between wilderness and civilization, and are sometimes linked with shape-shifting, revealing their crossing of the human frontier.[1] However, the fact is that he alone is able to be part of Artemis' coterie suggests that he alone goes deeper into the forest than his band of companions. He presents the goddess with a flower crown, saying:

> Goddess, for you I have twined this crown of flowers, gathered
> Fresh from a virgin meadow, where no shepherd dares
> To graze his flock, nor ever yet scythe swept,
> But bees thread the Spring air over the maiden meadow.
> There from the running stream Chastity waters the flowers;
> And those whose untaught natures Holiness claims entire
> May gather garlands there; and the impure may not.
> Dear Mistress, take this flowery band for your bright hair,
> Offered with reverent heart, I alone among mortals
> Enjoy this honor; I am your companion, speak with you,
> Hear your voice; only your face I do not see. (29-30).

Pure and detached from civic life, Hippolytus is able to meet the goddess in the heart of the wilderness.

If Artemis is wild nature, the matrix of becoming, that which lies beyond the human sphere, her love must hint or reflect something about his nature too, reflecting a non-human quality. Artemis, Lady of the Animals, was originally an outsider, according to Robert Pogue Harrison, "she belonged to those dark and inaccessible regions where wild animals enjoyed sanctuary from all human disturbance except that of the most intrepid hunters" (23). Hippolytus is one of that exclusive club of the "most intrepid." He is able to visit her virginal wilderness meadow, where he picks flowers to make garlands for her with but one limitation as a mortal: even he cannot see her actual face. But it is as if in experiencing that extraordinary proximity of the Sacred Other, Hippolytus has become a misfit when it comes to the human scene below the mountain, and so incurs the wrath of Aphrodite who would enmesh him in the web of the social, specifically by arousing the lust and passion of his stepmother, Queen Phaedra.[2]

Hippolytus has lived in that wild place where the masks of form fall and metamorphoses nakedly occur, that is at the heart of nature where kinship in the weave of life is revealed, including in its predator/prey cycles of transformation, (Harrison 29) a play often hidden in the human world of the polis so focused on political intrigues and gossip. Hippolytus is like a wild animal of a rare species, that will not survive long once brought down to the city. His mysterious beauty stirs and incites various envies and lusts, including the desire of the queen. Phaedra's lust leads to the web of deceit woven by her nurse who approaches Hippolytus and tells him of the queen's love for him; even as he reacts in disgust to his stepmother's incestuous offer, he swears he will tell no one about this, thus protecting the queen, even though he abhors her offer. Phaedra's outlash at her rejection, and then Theseus' wounded rage upon discovery of his queen's suicide ensnares the noble youth. Theseus believes his wife's suicide note, which claims that she was raped by Hippolytus, and refuses to believe his son, who maintains austere adherence to the oath he took to the nurse to not reveal the queen's advances to anyone, a strictness that comes across as part of his 'otherness' and traps him.

Theseus believing Phaedra's lie that his son has raped her (as she has claimed in her suicide note, as opposed to having rejected her passion) pronounces a curse upon his son in his blind rage, a power of cursing which had been given to him by Poseidon, and banishes him from the realm. Hippolytus takes off in his chariot accompanied by his friends; as they drive along the coast a huge wave breaks over the beach, and from the foam a monstrous bull emerges, panicking the horses who try to scramble up the rocky headland. So Hippolytus falls out and is dragged a long way over the rocks, his body badly mutilated. He is taken back to Theseus, nearly dead. There at the gate of the palace, the distraught king, reconciles with his son, as Artemis Herself appears and reveals the full story.

But Artemis has set him aside, he belongs to her: she proclaims that Asclepius will heal his death wound, and revive him into a kind of immortality, in her sylvan preserve remote beyond the reach of ordinary hunters and silviculturalists. Virgil writes, after Hippolytus "Had slaked with blood his father's vengeance rose to the starry/ Firmament. And breathed the air of Heaven, brought back/ To life by Diana's love, and the herbs of Aesculapius" (178 Book 7, lines 767-9). But she would still have to find a place to hide him from Zeus' anger at his escaping Hades.

A cult was set up for him at Troezen in the southern Peloponnesus, the city (and birthplace off Theseus) where most of the action of the play took place. Every year a festival was celebrated for him, in which as Frazer charmingly put it, "his untimely fate was mourned, with weeping and doleful chants by unwedded maids." It's a picture that resonates with other very different and overtly amorous parings of God/dess and Lover, including Adonis and Aphrodite, and also a wider assembly of beloved youths who by various means became immortalized from Hyacinthos to Antinous. Perhaps most surprising are the stories of how Artemis took him to Italy and set him up in the woods at Nemi, (the departure gate for Frazer's voracious armchair global ramblings) where Hippolytus was installed in the forest of the Golden Bough beside Lake Nemi, some fourteen miles from Rome, a volcanic crater lake in the hills beneath the

Alban Mount in the archaic Latin heartland (Grant). A local Italian cult must've been syncretized with that of Artemis and Hippolytus, and given a new origin myth. What an odd turn this story takes when grafted onto Italian soil. In Diana's sacred grove of Aricia at Nemi Hippolytus' name becomes Virbius. Ovid has Hippolytus say, regarding Diana that she "pondered long Whether for my new home to give me Crete or Delos... She placed me here {Nemi} and bade me put away the name that may recall that {horse} team of mine, Declaring, "You who were Hippolytus, shall now be Virbius.' Thenceforth my home is in this grove, one of the lesser gods..." (368).

In light of Hippolytus' horrid death, horses were forbidden from the sanctuary.[3]

And so Hippolytus, always liminal, lived on, lamented annually at Troezen, his shrine attended in Athens, and in the guise of Virbius on Latin soil, but also imaginatively roaming the deep woods under Artemis's care, hunting the deer, and plucking wildflowers in the wilderness. For he is in the abode of Potnia Theron, Homer's Lady of the Wild Animals, she who is the womb, the mother of all living things, who is both the hunted and the hunter, in a sustainable vision of the life cycle; a complex goddess, inaccessible, cruel and kind, even assisting in childbirth. In her realm I catch a glimpse of Hippolytus, a fleeting flash, seen through foliage: he tracks on the border of the phenomenal and the noumenal. A vision that today speaks to us of the very real limits of nature, of the need, as was known in the ancient past, for places that are beyond the utilization of humans, places that offering deep spiritual and imaginative resources.

Notes

[1]These outsider bands living in the woods, at least in the summer, are attested from many archaic Indo-European societies, and found mythically lurking in others. They are often associated with homoeroticism. For Ireland see Joseph Falaky Nagy's *The Wisdom of the Outlaw;* also of interest are Bernard Sergent's *Homosexuality in Greek Myth,* and Carlo Ginaburg's *The Night Battles.*

[2] This play shows what I see as an essential truth of polytheism, that with many deities, the individual may be caught between conflicting divine forces; a view of reality which seems much more realistic than that of monotheistic metaphysics.

[3] An alternate origin story, a literary one, told that Orestes and Iphigenia had brought the cult of Artemis to the Woods of Nemi, after fleeing with the image of the Goddess from her temple on the shore of the wild steppes of the Crimea. See Euripides' *Iphigenia in Aulis*.

Works Cited

Euripides. *Alcestis/Hippolytus/Iphigenia In Tauris*. Trans. Philip Vellacott. Harmondsworth: Penguin, 1953.

Frazer, Sir James George. *The Golden Bough*. 1 Vol. Abr. Ed. New York: Macmillan,1922.

Grant, Michael. *A Guide to the Ancient World: A Dictionary of Classical Place Names*. New York: Barnes & Noble, 1997.

Harrison, Robert Pogue. *Forests: The Shadow of Civilization*. Chicago: University of Chicago Press. 1992.

Ovid. *Metamorphoses*. Book XV. Trans. A.D. Melville. Oxford: Oxford University Press, 1986.

Vellacott, Philip. Introduction. *Alcestis/Hippolytus/Iphigenia In Tauris*. By Euripides.

Virgil. *The Aeneid*. Trans. C. Day Lewis. New York: Doubleday, 1953.

Artemis and the Cult of Antinous

by P. Sufenas Virius Lupus

One of the enduring aspects of Artemis' character, in mythological texts as well as cultic practice, is that she is fiercely independent, and goes about her activities without any reliance upon or strong identification with any male, whether god or mortal. Her rivalries and alliances with her younger brother Apollon come and go, and her possible interest in such figures as Orion is a minor tradition.[1] However, for the most part, her ability to stand on her own two feet, and more importantly, to run upon those feet swiftly, comes to the fore in a prevalent and obvious manner in much of the surviving literature concerning her.

While this is not an unusual situation for a goddess in the ancient world, modern pagans from non-reconstructionist religions might find this problematic, since in Wicca almost every goddess is expected to have a god as a consort (or perhaps son). This circumstance has made Artemis, and her Roman counterpart Diana, quite popular in some forms of feminist Wicca, including the eponymous Dianic movement. Given Artemis' close relationship to various women and the occasional nymph, some modern pagan women have taken Artemis or Diana as a profound divine exemplar of "sisterhood," even extending to the homoerotic senses of the term.

But this trend raises a further, and important, matter which could be leveled as a critique of many ancient mythologies: are there models of male and female interaction that do not involve either sexual connections, parenthood or other blood relationality, situations of rivalry (e.g. Hera's resentment of and enmity with Zagreus/Dionysos), or divine/mortal patronage (e.g. Athena and Odysseus)? Are there narratives or cultic occasions in which a male and female deity are "just friends"? There are precious few of these types of relation attested.

In this regard, the cultus to the hero/god Antinous is of particular note. Antinous' cult began in the year 130, after his death by drowning in the Nile while in the entourage of the Roman Emperor Hadrian, who was Antinous' elder lover (*erastes*). This cult is fascinating from a number of perspectives, and is marked by great variation and a diverse, promiscuous syncretism in the various locations in which it thrived.[2] While there were no human, nor divine, opposite sexed relationships of a romantic or sexual nature attested for Antinous in life nor in myth—with one possible exception, which will be discussed below—and the tendency with his cult does seem to have him honored singly in most instances, he does come into specific association with Diana in one location. Further, there are a few other occurrences which suggest a connection with either Diana, Artemis, or Selene, the lunar goddess who was sometimes syncretized to Artemis (especially in Romanized contexts, where Diana Luna is encountered).

The location in which Antinous and Diana are in specific, close association, in their sharing of a temple and being the deities to whom a collegium of devotees and "burial club" members were dedicated, is Lanuvium, a community not far from Rome, two miles north of the ancient site of Lake Nemi, the *Speculum Dianae* ("Diana's Mirror") where Diana Nemorensis had her sacred grove and the yearly priest-king guarding it (upon which Sir James George Frazer based a great deal of his theorizing in *The Golden Bough*). One relief sculpture from the site (which may or may not have been from their temple) shows Antinous with all the characteristics of the Roman god Silvanus, including most characteristically the *falx* or curved pruning knife that is one of the primary attributes of the god.[3] As Silvanus was, among other things, a god of hunting,[4] and did have attested homoerotic relationships (including with Cyparissos, who was thought to have been the guardian/keeper of a stag sacred to Artemis), it seems that he would have been an excellent deity to whom Antinous could have been syncretized and paired with the goddess Diana. The collegium's constitutional inscription has also survived, and gives many details, including the names of collegium members, the dates they held feasts for the deities (which included their birthdates—August 13 for Diana and November 27 for Antinous), and of what foods and drinks their feasts should consist.[5]

Nothing in what has been discovered thus far at Lanuvium suggests that Antinous and Diana were perceived in any sense to be related through amorous means. The reason why these two deities were chosen by this particular group of people for patronage of their society is uncertain, but many possibilities suggest themselves. Perhaps it was done to gain imperial favor, and the local goddess of great repute was previously acknowledged and simply augmented with the addition of the new male deity. It seems possible that the founders of the collegium were hunters and woodsmen, and therefore would have chosen deities for their protection in the afterlife who would have aided them and been recipients of their devotions during life. Perhaps this group of men were not interested in reproductive matters or promotion of fertility, and thus chose a known chaste goddess and an "uninterested" god from whom they might seek blessings. Any number of further possibilities could be suggested or explored....

From a modern viewpoint, both Diana and Antinous have great appeal for women and men who are homoerotically inclined, and thus pagans (whether reconstructionists or not) who are gay or lesbian might choose these deities as worthy of veneration. However, in a situation in which general misogyny amongst gay men, which can lead to bad relationships with lesbians, and in which a feminist (and sometimes separatist) critique of the patriarchy on the part of lesbians often ends up devaluing and excluding associations with males (including gay males), the "common interests" of Antinous and Diana at Lanuvium might indeed provide an excellent model for gay-lesbian cooperation and connection, on a far more visceral and practical level than the politically-correct propagation of inclusive monikers and acronyms that imply community when none exists. The divine model of Antinous and Diana might be an exemplar for queer males and females alike to reach out and build alliances directly with their sexually marginalized colleagues across the heterosexist gender divide.

A further piece of evidence from the ancient cultus suggests that Hadrian certainly, and Antinous possibly, did cultus to Diana during their lives, and thus it is possible that the interest in Diana on Antinous' part had precedent before his apotheosis. The "Boar Hunt" tondo, which is now on the Arch of Constantine but was once part of a conjectured Hadrianic hunting monument, has a figure in it which has been provisionally identified as Antinous, and (if the most common interpretation of the sequence of the tondi is correct) following this hunt, there is a dedication of the spoils to Diana.[6] Unfortunately, two figures in the Dianic tondo's faces have been obliterated: one is most certainly Hadrian, but the identification of the other is unknown. Whether such mortal cultic activity could earn one an association with a deity after one's death and deification is uncertain, but remains an intriguing possibility.

The Greek lunar goddess Selene is best known for her affections toward the mortal Endymion, for whom she interceded for his immortality, but in return for this unusual gift, he was to remain forever asleep. Some Roman period sources connect Diana to the goddess Luna, who was Rome's equivalent of the Greek Selene. This somewhat problematizes the earlier suggestions of Artemis/Diana's independence from male romantic relationships, and yet, it is an important issue to consider in the present case, because of the witness of a fragmentary papyrus hymn from Oxyrynchus dating to the late third century CE (made as part of a eulogy for the occasion of the Emperor Diocletian's accession to the principate, c. 285 CE), which was discovered in the early 1990s.[7] A continuous portion of this text runs as follows:

> I revere, Narcissus, your shadowy reflection; I shed a tear for Hyacinthus, who grasped the cruel discus; I pity your hunting of the wild beast, Adonis. Yet the meadow of

Antinous and his lovely new flower envy not pool, not fatal discus, not boar. The nymphs began to crown their tresses with the flower named after Antinous, which to this day preserves the mighty spear of the hunter. Into the Nile he hurried for purification of the blood of the lion, but the Moon [Selene] upon more brilliant hopes bade him shine as a star-like bridegroom and garlanding the new light with a circle she took him for her husband.

In addition to making the reference to the flower named for Antinous (and thus his comparison to various slain youths who became flowers or plants—amongst which is Adonis, who is elsewhere syncretized to Antinous,[8] and we also recall the boar hunt tondo mentioned above in relation to the boar mentioned here that was responsible for Adonis' death), it seems that the implication here is that Antinous' apotheosis was, in some sense, due to Selene's direct action, and in fact her love for him. Antinous was regarded to have become a star after his death (very likely in association with a celestial anomaly that happened in late January of 131, about three months after his death),[9] and there is further evidence from a Christian critic of the Antinoan cult, Tatian the Assyrian (died c. 172 CE), that Antinous was regarded in some circles as being the "face in the moon."[10]

The final connection between Artemis and Antinous is conjectural, but nonetheless fascinating to consider. Hadrian's activity in Ephesus is well known, and he most certainly patronized the cult of the great goddess Artemis in that city, in addition to founding sacred athletic games there.[11] Ulrike Outschar has made the intriguing suggestion that perhaps the Sebasteion at Ephesus, a building of uncertain use and purpose, may have been a hero-shrine to Antinous.[12] Ephesian honoring of Antinous is evidenced by statuary found there, as well as coinage, but in absence of any inscriptions indicating that this building may have included such functions, it must remain an enticing but unproven speculation.

A few thoughts suggest themselves in conclusion to this exploration of the connections between these two deities. It would seem that there are two possible, generalized relationships that Artemis was known to have with people of the opposite sex (who were not her direct divine relations): the situation I would characterize as the "sin of Actaeon," and that which I'd classify as the "triumph of Orion." In the former, a prospective mate, seducer, or lover of Artemis/Diana comes forward seeking lustful ends, which would considerably compromise Artemis' independence, and in turn the offending male is utterly destroyed. In the latter, however, a worthy possible mate (or perhaps "just someone to talk with") who distinguishes himself as an excellent hunter and heroic personage, is loved from afar by the goddess, and when he meets a tragic end, is heroized and given a celestial memorial. It seems that Antinous does not commit the sin of Actaeon, but that perhaps in some interpretations, Artemis/Diana's favor was inferred or even expounded upon in relation to the events which occurred with Antinous' death and the astronomical miracles which followed it. Not only does this provide a potentially illuminating and insightful model for friendly, non-sexual relations between the male and female genders amongst pagans in the modern period (no matter what their sexual orientation might happen to be), but it provides insight into the "type" of male which Artemis, if she had her choice about matters, would find attractive and worthy to take into her patronage, her entourage, and perhaps even her more intimate congresses.

---

[1] See e.g. Michael P. Speidel, *Mithras-Orion* (Leiden: E. J. Brill, 1980). A further fascinating possibility for interaction with Artemisian priestesses and males occurs in Celtic (specifically Galatian) contexts, with Artemis in some sense being a "sovereignty goddess" whose representative—the priestess—mates with the rightful king of a territory, but insures the ruin of an unrightful ruler. This model is exhibited in the story of Sinatus, Sinorix, and the Artemisian priestess Camma, as related in Plutarch and Polyaenus; see John T. Koch and John Carey (eds.), *The Celtic Heroic Age:* Literary Sources for Ancient Celtic Europe & Early Ireland & Wales, Fourth Edition (Aberystwyth and Andover: Celtic Studies Publications, 2003), pp. 40-42.

² See Royston Lambert, *Beloved and God: The Story of Hadrian and Antinous* (New York: Viking, 1984); and, more recently, several chapters in Caroline Vout, *Power and Eroticism in Imperial Rome* (Cambridge: Cambridge University Press, 2007).
³ Anthony R. Birley, *Hadrian the Restless Emperor* (New York and London: Routledge, 2001), pp. 284-286.
⁴ See Peter F. Dorcey, *The Cult of Silvanus: A Study in Roman Folk Religion* (Leiden: E. J. Brill, 1992).
⁵ Mary Beard, John North, and Simon Price (eds./trans.), *Religions of Rome, Volume 2: A Sourcebook* (Cambridge: Cambridge University Press, 1998), pp. 292-294. Unfortunately, other cultic activities are not detailed, which illustrates one of the most appealing and yet confounding aspects of the ancient Antinoan cultus' remains: exact dates and details of the relatively recent deity's honoring are fairly easy to come by, but the details of actual activities, rituals, and texts employed remain quite elusive.
⁶ Birley, p. 284; Mary Taliafero Boatwright, *Hadrian and the City of Rome* (Princeton: Princeton University Press,), pp. 192, 195-196. Antinous certainly appears in the "Departure" tondo, and it is also conjectured that he appears in the "Lion Hunt" tondo.
⁷ J. R. Rea (ed./trans.), *The Oxyrynchus Papyri*, Vol. 63 (London: Egypt Exploration Society, 1996), pp. 1-17.
⁸ See Wolfgang Dieter Lebek, "Ein Hymnus auf Antinoos," *Zeitschrift für Papyrologie und Epigraphik* 12 (1973), pp. 101-137; for a non-academic translation of this, see P. Sufenas Virius Lupus, *The Phillupic Hymns* (Eugene: Bibliotheca Alexandrina, 2008), p. 227, with notes pp. 269-270.
⁹ Rea, pp. 14-15.
¹⁰ *Pros Hellenas* Chapter 10.
¹¹ Birley, pp. 181, 222; Mary Taliafero Boatwright, *Hadrian and the Cities of the Roman Empire* (Princeton: Princeton University Press, 2000), pp. 95-100.
¹² Ulrike Outschar, "Zur Deutung des Hadrianstempels an der Kuretenstrasse," in Herwig Friesinger and Fritz Krinzinger (eds.), *100 Jahre österreichische Forschungen in Ephesos, Akten des Symposions Wien 1995* (Vienna: Verlag der Österreichischen Akademie der Wissenschaften, 1999), pp. 443-448.

Finding a Shrine's Home

by Allyson Szabo

My family are hunters. We're not terribly experienced, but we do our best to be responsible keepers of our property. Large flocks of wild turkey and vast herds of deer are destructive to both our property and themselves, and so we do our part in keeping populations to a good level. We raise much of our own chicken, and often buy a local pig or part of a cow to avoid paying grocery store managers to maintain a system we disagree with.

My partner Amo was hunting turkey. He was watching them across the field when they startled and disappeared into the forest up the hill on our property. He took a shot, a freak shot, probably one he should not have taken. When the mass of turkeys was gone, what remained was a small herd of four deer. Since no turkey dropped from the sky, and all four deer were standing calmly, he guessed that he had missed everything. He watched, consternated, when the deer followed the turkeys into the forest.

His instincts got the better of him. He decided to go track the turkeys and deer, just in case he had nicked an animal and it was suffering. We're not ones to leave an animal suffering if we can help it. He went far beyond where he felt his shot could have reached, not sure why he continued on but certain he should do so. When he reached the far end of the field, he found a small blood trail, and then the deer herself.

After assuring himself that the doe was dead, not suffering in any way, he returned to fetch me. "I didn't get your turkey, but I need help. I dropped a deer." Oops. Not in season. Still, we are not ones to waste, and she was already dead. There was nothing to do but deal with the issue, and where we live, there's a bit of leeway when it comes to 'varmints' on your own property. So I threw on jeans and muck boots, and took off across the field, ready to do what was necessary.

I got there, and could tell immediately that it was a doe, and she was pregnant. I had mixed emotions as I knelt beside her, my hands on her cooling body, saying prayers to the gods, and especially to Artemis. We needed the meat, so I didn't regret that part at all, but we do try to stick to males unless it's doe season. Amo was upset with himself, but we had the situation before us, and we would take care of it.

I prayed. I thanked Artemis especially, for bringing the bounty to our table and our larder. I thanked the deer for her sacrifice, and apologized for taking her at such a precious time. Then the time had come; we had to gut her. You do that in the field, and it's traditional to leave the innards as an offering to the local wildlife. So we split her, silently and swiftly, and Amo held her open so I could reach within to clean her out.

The first part to exit her abdominal cavity was her uterus. Confirmation that she was pregnant was right before my eyes as double sacks came out. I cursed myself and Amo for this, because twins are wonderful for the deer herds, and we want the does who can produce them to stay alive. I was angry at both of us for taking a shot when there was a chance of hitting a deer.

When I had time, I took the uterus and split it open. I needed to know. I had to see for myself the damage we had done. I was taken aback when I discovered not two, but three small bodies within. One tiny body was within its own sack, and it was perfect and beautiful. The other sack contained two deer, and one was horribly misshapen. At that time, I whispered another prayer of thanks to Artemis, because this doe would not have survived the birth of her offspring, and it's unlikely the offspring would have survived, either. A clean death by bullet was much more merciful than the slow and messy death in painful childbirth. After that moment of fervent prayer, I took the small bodies and put them by their mother's head. I laid them as if for a funeral pyre, and commended them to Artemis.

I will be putting my shrine to Artemis on that spot. I am taking it as a sign that it is the right place for it, and that she meant us to find both her deer and the small glen she died in. It was a clean shot. Amo got her right in the front chest, collapsing her lungs almost instantly, and she didn't suffer at all. She just got three bounds, from field to the glen, before she dropped.

It was a moment of very raw power. We have been living a somewhat rural lifestyle for a few years now, and I have been lucky enough to offer both blood and meat sacrifices to the gods on a couple of occasions each year. This was different. This was not an animal bred for the slaughter, raised with love, yes, but with the purpose of sacrifice to my freezer. This deer was free, and wild. She was stately, and large, and incredibly beautiful. I feel that I am truly blessed, both by Artemis and the other gods, to be able to participate in this way with the nature of our land. I have never worshiped Artemis before, other than as "one of the Olympians," but this was a clear omen. Being the guiding force behind a mercy killing, even without knowing, tells me that we did right.

I'm not vain, though. I also took this as a sign to be wary. This time, this accident led to the death of a deer out of season, a pregnant doe, and she could have been ready to give birth to healthy offspring. This is a lesson, and we are paying heed to it.

It was difficult, very emotionally painful, placing those little bodies beside their mother's head. No matter how reverent we were, we caused their death and I take responsibility for that. Yet, despite the death of the deer there, the glen feels powerful, and consecrated. I will clear space, and set up a full shrine there, even if it is a small one. Tending it will be a chore, requiring abstinence from certain activities that I enjoy heartily, but I also have the help of a small cadre of teen girls. I feel honored to be leading them in this worship, in this reverent tending of the shrine.

Artemis is known as a goddess of hunting, of wilderness and hills, and of animals. She is also the bringer of swift death, and all these things were highlighted dramatically in this episode. One of her epithets is *elaphêbolos*, meaning stag killer, which seems most appropriate.

To Artemis

by Sannion

Artemis, swift-footed, virgin huntress, racing through the wilds,
heart beating in her slender chest with excitement for the chase.
The hint of a smile turns up her lips as she scents her prey's fear upon the air,
the deer rushing headlong through the thicket, desperate to escape Leto's proud daughter.
She it is, the doubling goddess, who has never known the touch of man,
but keeps the company of athletic girls and wild beasts,
who despite her fondness for the chase, is the one who nurtures all young,
human and animal alike, and stands guard at their birth.
She takes the fawn to her breast, nursing it like a maenad on the hill,
and watches as it takes its first, faltering steps. Under her keen gaze
the deer grows strong, knowing only joy in its innocent sport.
Yet she it is who draws the bow, and spills their blood upon the loamy soil,
dual natured mother of the wild.

Analyzing the Role of Artemis the Huntress

by Lykeia

The stealthy goddess hunts her prey, no tender babe clinging to its mother's side. She hunts the fruitful mature animal, keeping it within her sight as she pursues it through the forest. The forest, the home of the living things she hunts to their ends.

Artemis is a goddess familiar to anyone who has picked up a book on mythology. Before all other things she is most easily recognized as this huntress figure. She is the goddess at the back door in the wild places at the edges of civilization. We often view her from a relative distance of safety, to applaud the strength of the huntress, the freedom and necessity within the natural world, but a world that so many no longer consider themselves fully a part of. Instead they feel separated from it, mere spectators watching the wilds slowly dwindle away. But when we are confronted with her directly we have the opportunity to acknowledge the terrifying ferocity that drives the wild animals to flee. This untamable and uncontrollable energy that is always present regardless of where we are at in the world that pushes at us and drives us toward our potential, the very thing that we need the most.

To clarify, when we think of hunting we are usually not thinking of some random exercise without direction or goal, but rather a purposeful fulfilling of a need whether it is physical, emotional or spiritual. There are those who still subsist by hunting and have that direct link between prey and predator, and the sacredness that lies within that relationship. Their physical need fulfilled by this activity can be directly connected to their spiritual well-being and may play out in emotional and social venues. However, for many hunting is not a physical necessity and could be considered impractical. This is particularly true among areas of dense human population. Instead hunting takes on forms of spiritual or emotional bonding, rites of passage, and probably most commonly seeking the object of our desire. This may be more evident in the different ways we use the word "hunt."

Photographers stalk and hunt, and often through some very exotic environments and among some dangerous creatures. There are those who laughingly refer to bargain hunting. Even finding the perfect mate has become characterized as a certain type of hunting for many people. This driving force often speaks to us through our desires or fears in order to satisfy a deep-seated need. This desire is a demanding impulse. So then would it be correct to think of Artemis in her guise as huntress strictly in the sense of a of a goddess who is in charge of hunting animals? Furthermore, would this measure up to what we know of how the ancient Greeks lived? Or how most people live today? I am certain that at a time there was a majority of people who relied on such a subsistence relationship, but this long ceased to be the norm for a great many even within the ancient period. It wouldn't seem likely that Artemis would have such little direct influence on people as a huntress if that was all she was as a huntress of or if she were limited to just a huntress in the realms of literal wilderness. Not when civilization and culture was such an important facet of ancient Greek life, and is a prominent emphasis in most modern cultures today.

In our discussion of civilization, and thus humanity itself, we must take into consideration what part the natural world's influence plays on the survival of human civilization itself. First land must be prepared in a manner that is conducive to human settlement. This often involves the clearing and preparations for a foundation despite inhabiting threats. This comes with the acknowledgement that we run the risk of our efforts being swallowed back into the wilderness that it arose from. It is our relationship with this wilderness that permits us to go forward or can entangle us in the end. In order to advance as a species we needed a driving force to help us evolve so that we could reason, effectively communicate, and anticipate the future. An element within nature pushed us to progress within the natural world, within the wilderness until finally we were able to be pushed out of our nest and develop culturally and spiritually. This is not to say that all instances of this progress are an exact mirror of each other, because spiritually and culturally rich peoples who live in a manner appropriate for their culture and environment will have wide variances throughout the world. We cannot judge any culture or civilization as superior or inferior. We are all fully developed humans with layers of social and spiritual complexity.

However, progress is not always pleasant. We as a species often do not deal with it in a balanced fashion that safeguards the rest of the natural world, which can have some dire consequences for us. After all, we are dependent on the nurturing capacity of the natural world. We are dependent on the forests for their medicines, air, and habitats for our non-human siblings on this planet. We are dependent on the restorative processes of the wild to provide us with a healthy environment so that we in turn have healthy bodies and lives. For those who believe in reincarnation, we recognize our kinship with the other inhabitants of the natural world. Even biologically we have to recognize the interdependence and relationships between all of Earth's species and the cyclic necessity that we share.

And so there is Artemis drawing up the babes into her arms. She holds the infant beasts of the woods protectively in her care, and welcoming into the world the newest of each species. She is loving even as she is threatening and terrifying. And she takes joy in her purpose, her sacred role in nature. Likewise she can tend and care for human civilization, keep us safe from that which we are not yet prepared to deal with. Like a mother she defends and protects us, but delivers what we need for our growth and development. She is nurturing while at the same time she is armed with her arrows.

What does this mean individually? How does Artemis relate to each person in such a manner? As individuals we are all progressing at our own rate. The scale of humanity is but an average between the different states of progression among billions of people. We all have this driving force, this elemental pushing, that spurs our souls. It can be overwhelming or frightening, and sometimes lead to disappointment as you struggle to fulfill that need; at the same time it can fill you with energy and give you a sense of purpose. We aim toward our potential, like an arrow notched, and we only need the power behind the bow to send us flying along to the heights of what we can be. And yet like the little animals of the woods she spreads out her protective arms over each of us when it is most needed.

Artemis hunts us each individually, indeed pushing all of humanity, the endorphin-filled chase through our lives. We walk, we run, we rest and sometimes we may stumble but she is always there pursuing us, speaking to our soul and most internal being. She prepares the journey, she plots the way through the forest that is most effective, and she wields her torch in the darkest part of night to brighten the road.

We can all readily say Hail Artemis Agrotera!

Hunting the Snow

by Paul Derrick

Deepest winter.

Kheimon holds the world with icy fingers,
Her dark wings beating, chasing, smothering life.

And yet – something stirs. The Lady of the Hunt
Will not be denied – not by cold or crushing silence.
A woman of infinite grace, Artemis
Treads with bare feet the snow-covered forest,
Stalking, watching ... waiting.

A snowstorm rages
She hardly blinks.
Frost's chilling claws reach for Her
She dismisses them with a turn of the head.
Her breath turns to ice before Her eyes
But She waits not in vain.

A stag,
Milk-white, imperceptible against the snow.
But yet, She perceives it, and
Moving from Her position She readies an arrow on Her bow.
Treading silently She approaches Her prey.

The creature turns, sees, and makes to run –
But the stag, even the trees themselves
Are moved by the Goddess' astonishing beauty.
Hunter and hunted remain still,
The Lady silkily drawing her bow –
The stag flees.

Abandoning pretence, Artemis runs also.

She revels in the chase, Her laughter floating on the freezing wind.
The animal tears through the forest,
Death always in the corner of its mind.

At last, exhausted, it stops, and
Artemis, exhilarated, releases Her bowstring.
The arrow silently glides through the air,
Making contact with the creature precisely as She knew it would.

The stag falls to the ground. The Huntress approaches,
And kneels beside it, letting out a single, warrior's cry.
She weeps for Her victim, yet also rejoices,
Thanking the woods and the Earth for her bounty.

Gaia was kind today. Such a kill is rare in these months -
But Her chance will come again.

The Reflecting Pool

by Michael Routery

Ames C. Timmons hopped into his SUV, after loading his guns and dogs. The pack was frothing already, über-excited at the outing; Ames was chomping himself to get out of town and up into the mountains. It was the season and he was going to get his rage out; he'd worked out, in fact, he worked out six days a week: Monday was for abs, Tuesday for legs, Wednesday for chest, Thursday for arms, Friday was back and Saturday, chest again. He'd put on a lot of bulk, but there was nothing like the thrill of hunting. He jammed on brakes and then skidded across a lane, simultaneously shrieking, "get off the road, motherfucker," giving the finger, and then slamming the accelerator into the free lane. Soon the last house had been passed, the last office blocks, the kind that sat out there, abandoned looking a few miles from town past the Walmart. He and the dogs skimmed along through cow country, and headed uphill; he took a swig from his thermos. "Boys we're gonna get ourselves a deer today." Too bad Ken and Brett couldn't come, but what the hey, he had plenty of canine company—the best friends and all. The clichés are true, he told himself.

He observed his biceps in the mirror, bulging out his shirtsleeves; he'd once been a barista at Starbucks, weak shit that, who'd taken it from Karla. "Karla, now I should've seen it coming," he told the dogs. "Fucking lesbo bitch." Karla had taken him for everything, had opened up a river of blood in his heart and then taken off— had been slinking around behind his back even when they lived together, she a student, working on her nursing degree. Then she left him for Diane. His blood throttled with the quick turns, as he zigzagged up through the deep green cool forest, exhilaration rising as if he was ripping open a Christmas or birthday package. The dark silent Doug fir and cedar forest pressed against his vision. Yeah, revenge was sweet, he thought, that's what

Reverend Rick taught. Jesus was no queer limpwrist crap like he'd been taught as a kid in dad's nice church; no way, he was macho, he took out and slammed back, he was fight club. "Shit, yeah," he shouted out to the dogs, who were making heavy breathing noises.

Later he launched off onto a small road, and lurched into 3-wheel drive. It led up to a little-used trail; soon there was nothing but a narrow patch of gravel before the wheels, on which the Suburban bounced mightily, jarring his knees and joints as Diane hovered tauntingly in his mind. How could that majestic shelf, those forces of nature be off limits to dudes, and the way she dressed, those plunging necklines. He remembered when he just thought she was Karla's poet friend from the college. He would've dismissed her, but that coal black hair, those witch eyes, the v-necks, and the tats, that only led you to peek further and speculate, making men hunger, for turning men into drooling fools was her game. The vehicle bounded hard over a rock that had fallen in the road. One of the dogs, Chuck, barked loud, and Ames realized his crotch bulged out. Yeah, he'd have loved to have thrown Diane over the couch and slammed her good—he dreamt of it to tell the truth, that'd teach the cock-tease, the lipstick lesbo slam poet. Reverend Rick said not to take any shit, but you couldn't go and get messed up with the law; it was a hard condition, at least it was kind of comforting to realize just how fucked we all are. It's the human condition, God made it that way and there's no arguing it, humans are just deep shit, corrupt from the beginning. But why did God make us anyway, then? Ames couldn't help but wonder. Maybe someday he could hang around at MileHigh after service with Rick.

Ames drove on until the road dwindled away. He was beyond the national forest hunting zone, and at the entrance to the protected wilderness area. He didn't even bother to read the sign with the notice about all that. Actually, it made him feel full of win to unload his rifle. He trotted onto the trail, breaking the law; but again Diane and Karla helicoptered in his mind's vision like two hornet fairies from some cartoon, mocking. Diane and Karla cavorting with each other; Karla's newfound veganism; her accusations against him, calling him a spoiled faux-something other; seeing them arm in arm in the café by the campus, where Diane performed her spoken word shit; Diane's van, with the 'save the old growth' bumper stickers. Oh yeah, girls, I will have a present for you! He whistled and his dogs bounded about him, Sunny and Chuckie and Brigand, his big bad Dobies; they understood his bloody heart, they commiserated, they licked his hands, right now, just excited to be in these cool green woods, full of critters.

Somewhere high above a raven broke the silence, making Ames realize just how quiet it was up here, like a safety glass wall that could be shattered only with difficulty. His blood was pumping, his heart pounding, as they hurried up the steep and muddy trail, splotches of moist dirt spattering his boots and his jeans. The dogs took off at some sound, it was late in the year, and cold; there wasn't much activity, yet the forest towered above him, the trees higher and higher, and as if waiting for something. He speculated that if he was lucky he'd get one of the rare elk or mountain goats that lived in the heights as he broke through into a rocky open area and in the distance saw a high notched peak like a castle.

Man, there could be bears up here, he thought; he shuddered involuntarily, his dogs super-alert, twitching. The silence gripped him, but it wasn't really silence, there was the sound of the wind quietly moving the branches, some bug noise too, and he could hear his heart. Ames was really sweating, he raked his sleeve across his brow. Startled, he saw a man coming down the trail. "Are those your hounds?" he asked. His eyes seemed to look through his skin, penetrating, drilling into his inside spaces, places he barely knew about himself. "There's no hunting up here," he added quietly, almost a whisper, as he went on, wearing a weird leather coat. And there were leaves in his long hair—maybe he lived up here, but he looked too, healthy or something, Ames thought. He launched back on the trail, the weirdest thing being the dogs had ignored the man. What if he reported him? It would take him a long time, but still it pricked at him, anxiety souring in the pit of his belly.

As he launched out across an open meadow, the sun directly overhead, surprisingly hot, the dogs yowled at the edge of a grove of thick dark conifers stood. Ames headed for its tempting shade. Within the sun was blotted out, the shadows closed tightly around him. Diane and Karla together rose in his thoughts — they'd love this place he thought, a tiny lake like a jewel snuggled in the center of the tiny dark-wooded valley. A good spot for a break, he thought. Oddly as he looked at the aquamarine waters, a terrible sadness surged in his heart; his eyes watered, misted over, with all that had happened, all that had gone wrong. He felt torn as if held under cold knifelike claws. They tugged at his heart like in those nature programs where the lions struggle over the choicest cuts. What if he just let go and fell into the pain, what if falling was healing? Karla said that, but what if you never got up? He remembered his father, always zipped up, disapproving of his recklessness. Ames wrenched himself forward.

The waters of the lake were strangely opalescent now, a fog rising from the surface tension. The dogs had fallen silent, but he realized he was not alone – there were some nude girls there, or maybe he was hallucinating; they were just too beautiful. One rose tall – his mind was playing games, he thought, as he slipped clumsily into the water toward her; it was icy and tingly and curiously fizzy. His mind failed at the sight of the tall one's reflection, yet his eyes tried, even though her beauty hurt like staring at the sun, no, like moonlight but impossibly bright.

Pain shivered through him, his muscles wrenched, his body was jerking spasmodically, it was like he was growing or elongating. Grasping for straws he wondered if the steroids he'd been taking could cause this. He'd tried to call to the dogs, but his tongue fought him, his tongue squirreled and churned inside his mouth, and his scalp burst with wrenching pain.

In terror he looked for his reflection in the terrible water, but shining back darkly was a half-man half-deer, antlers erupting from its head, tears of blood dripping onto its muzzle. With one last spurt of will he tried to break from that vision, but this new body had triumphed. It leapt with an incredible bounce in the legs, all four of them, as he tried to scream, but a sound like a bell tore from the throat, as the dogs arrived.

He raised his head toward them, tried to greet them with his eyes (you know me, guys!) but they were jumping at him, pulling at his throat, teeth clenching savagely, greedily. Prone on that piney ground, red moisture pooled all about, dripping into the soil, and there were terrible whispers, and the land thrummed all around him in insect and birdsong, and more terrible songs of unrecognizable words, and the wind on the rocks. Laughter rippled about him as the last of his breath exhaled, and he joined with it, his terrible loneliness surrendered.

My Experiences with Artemis

by Melia Suez

I've been having some interesting experiences with an Artemis – but she isn't the Artemis that I remember reading of in the Greek myths. You know, the aggressive, ball-busting bitch who would tear you apart as soon as pass by you.

If anything she is closer to, and I hesitate to say it, Wicca's view of the Goddess. By that I mean she seems more all encompassing than the myths have led me to believe her to be. She is the maiden in that she is a virgin in the old sense: belonging to no man, independent, whole and complete. She is there at the beginning, at birth. She believes in loving freely and wherever you will. She is laughter and dance. She is running wild and following instinct. While she is commonly portrayed as a maiden, she has much more to her than that narrow categorization, since she also has characteristics that are commonly attributed in the general pagan mindset with the mother and the crone. She is nurturing. She is the disciplinarian who will give you a kick in the ass if you need it. She has her mysteries. She is intuition and knowledge. She is the hunter and is there when life ends.

***

One day during meditation, I found myself faced with a stag that seemed large yet small at the same time. I was given the impression that I was to climb onto its back. I was incredulous, thinking that I'm a little big and heavy for that stag's back. I was snorted at and got on anyway. The stag started to run and run and run. At first I was worried about how to hold on, but I caught the thought that I wasn't coming off no matter what until it was time so that I might as well enjoy the ride. So I closed my eyes. It was like being on a motorcycle but without the noise only the wind rushing through my hair. It was quite relaxing. When the stag stopped, I found myself in a meadow where a glowing woman was laying in the sun, basking in its warmth. She was wearing something loosely draped around the hips, snug around the chest yet short enough to make movement easy. She had on tall boots and appeared to have a short cloak underneath her. Her hair was dark, wavy and a little shorter than shoulder length.

She held her arms open to me and I laid down with my head cushioned on her arm. She pulled me close and said to cry it out. So I did. I cried hysterically and until I could cry no more. As I settled back down, I realized that that I couldn't hear her breathe. I opened my eyes out of curiosity and found myself laying against an oblong mound, covered in grass and wildflowers.

What was I crying over? A failed romance that, two years later, still burdens my heart.

***

During another meditation, I was in a meadow. A stag appeared and I was given the impression that I needed to follow it. It led me down a narrow trail into a large forest. I remember at one point, I stumbled (clumsy even there) only to find the stag under my arm to keep me from falling. On it led me to a small clearing with a clear pond that was surrounded almost completely by flowers and bushes. I was given the impression that this was Artemis' bathing pond and that I was to strip and get in. I was shocked as it seemed like blasphemy or defilement to do so. The stag stood behind me blocking my path, not pushing but clear that the only way for me to go was into the pond. Suddenly I knew why I was here. The purpose of this dip was to return me to myself. I had invested so much of myself in my failed romance that I had lost something vital. My sense of self, my sense of individuality. I was out of balance. This dip was to start the process of returning to who I was. There was no feeling of judgment, only a feeling of timeliness. I did get in and the pond was short of being uncomfortably cool. By the time I was starting to really enjoy the water, I was encouraged to continue my journey. In front of me a path opened up and the next guide on my journey was waiting.

This meditation was the first time that I had any indication that Artemis had an interest in me. I continue to explore this relationship with her, with no idea where it will go. I only know that she is much different than I naively believed.

Lady of the Cedar

by Jennifer Lawrence

How odd: that I thought of you each time
I breathed the scent of juniper,
But didn't know that it was your holy tree,
Until I came across that reference entirely by accident.
Walking through the forest on a summer's eve,
I can see the tears of golden resin
On the outstretched branches (reaching to embrace me),
Tears beyond price from the wood that weeps for your return.
Artemis Kedreatis, Artemis Hymnia,
There once was a temple at Orkhomenos
– No more than ruins now –
Which I may never see; they kept your image in the crook
Of a tree there, and under that tree, with its red-gold berries,
Your priestess might have sat, on a summer eve
Not too different from this one,
Smelling that sweet perfume that I smell now.
I am no virgin, nor have been for many years,
And likewise my time of childbirth is long over.
Even so, forgive me if, once in a while,
I linger by the juniper tree,
Breathing in that scent,
And imagine myself joyously in service to you.

Artemis at Eleusis

by Lykeia

There is a light upon the road
Where the twin torches raised
Lead in a cyclic dance of life
Nodding from their two seats
The double arcs of pointed light.
The radiance of moon and sun
Dancing with their governance
Mark out the timely span
Bound beneath nature's law
Upon the cultivated land.
Souls upon Demeter's road
Where she waits, poppy crowned
In one hand the flow of seed
In the other the grain of gold
A journey the white dogs keep
Loving guardians of loyalty
Advancing to the huntress' lead,
And bright sounding Hekate Skilakitis,
To the favored hunt of Artemis .
There the leader of the hounds
Child of solid earth and moving sea
Whom the nymphs of two planes
Keep in swift-footed company
She dances before them all
Across the shadow bridge
Where seven pillars stand
Of frightful gaze that does not deter
The coiled path of the running dogs.
On the road traveling between
The sweet water and the sea
Along the sacred road
The tempered souls travel

As each year marks its round
Their curving road circling around
Like a labyrinth's hidden path
To the altar before the steps
Of the greater gate that awaits
To welcome you initiates.
She stands before the blossom
The flower opened to bloom
With perfect numbered petals firm
And two torches mark the presence
Of where the bright twins reside,
Between their flames the sacrifice
Purified by the grasp of the sea
A mother sacrificed for her progeny
A death to be reborn
The seed that drops
The egg born to new beginning
Before the great gates of Eleusis.
And as a girl, like a bride,
Gives her childhood final respect
To lay her girdle at the altar
Of loud-laughing Artemis,
Here the old misty gowns are laid
Tattered and shorn from their travail
Before the great gates of Eleusis.

Artemis and Dionysos: Antithesis and Synthesis

by Thista Minai

I've long believed that the root of the clash (for lack of a better word) between Artemis and Dionysos comes from the fact that They are each Gods of freedom and transition – only Artemis approaches it by knowing boundaries well and thus being able to cross over or through them, while Dionysos destroys the boundaries altogether. Reading *Written in Wine* [a devotional anthology for Dionysos] recently has helped me to understand this quite a bit more, so here are some of my thoughts on the subject.

The first thing that struck me when I started *Written in Wine* was how similar Dionysos and Artemis really are. People would speak of turning to Dionysos for the exact same things that I would turn to Artemis for, and the effect they described was very similar to the effect Artemis has on me. Nevertheless, the second thing that struck me was how antithetical Dionysos and Artemis are. They go about things in such incredibly different ways that even though They accomplish the same end, They can't – or perhaps simply don't – coexist in the same place.

Artemis and Dionysos are both filled with contradictions. The God of madness and destruction is also a God of growth and vegetation. The Goddess of hunting is also the Goddess who protects animals. We all know how these are two sides of the same coin, necessary for each other. The ways in which Artemis and Dionysos contradict each other, though, don't seem to be complementary in that way. I think this is best illustrated in the type of wildness one experiences in the company of either.

My limited understanding of the wildness of Dionysos is that it is (eventually, anyway, as seen through the eyes of a non-devotee) complete madness. The ultimate result is liberation and thus being better able to fully express and understand one's self, but the path to get there involves at least temporarily but completely losing yourself in Dionysian madness, just fully letting go. There is no control, and the point perhaps *is* to lose control. There is almost no self in it at all, just ecstatic frenzy.

The wild dances of Artemis are similarly liberating, but there is no loss of consciousness (for lack of a better expression) involved. Her dance is wild and unfettered but self-aware – not in an angsty, self-conscious sort of way, but in a way where She could see a deer nearby and hunt it and shoot it down without missing a step in the dance. It's a wild awareness. Artemis says "Look, within yourself. There's a beast inside you. Know it and be wild. Be the beast and know it as yourself." There is never any point where you are separated from yourself. The boundary between you and beast is still there, and yet through Her lessons of wildness you become able to cross from one side of that boundary to the other at will, in effect integrating that beast into yourself. She shows us how to welcome and embrace being wild and beastly without ever letting go of our self control. That wild freedom concurrent with control is one of Artemis' internal paradoxical contradictions. As Sannion explains it,

> *I've always felt that a fundamental key to understanding Artemis (and relatedly her brother) is through the archer, the bow, the intense focus and concentration necessary to shoot straight and clear. Kind of a Zen thing. You don't lose yourself, but you become aware of things to a degree you normally aren't – paradoxically through the narrowing of focus. It shuts out all the background noise, the internal static, until there is just you, aiming the arrow, and the victim whose every movement you are so keenly conscious of.*

In fact, Artemis is very much about boundaries and transitions both, and that's a 'two sides of the same coin' sort of complementary contradiction. Know both sides clearly, know exactly where the line is, and then you can cross from one side to the other easily, and even walk the fine line itself. Her temples were often at liminal areas, space between or on the edge. She presided over transitions, but these were all rituals where someone went from one state to another. There would often be wild chaos in the middle (e.g., the whipping of Orthia, or the *arkteia* of Brauronia) but even in this wildness there would be no confusion of which state was which or where they were. Before you were one thing, in the middle you are wild, and after you are something else. The lines are permeable, and there is even often space of liminal wildness in the middle, but the lines are also always clear.

Dionysos, on the other hand, seems to be about blurring those lines or destroying them altogether. I can't go into depth about it because I don't understand Him as well, but it seems to me that in His madness, you're not really sure where each side is, or if there are even sides anymore at all. Perhaps part of the point of this is to illustrate the necessity of boundaries by showing the chaos that emerges in their absence. Even so, I think that right away this makes it pretty clear why Artemis and Dionysos generally don't go so well together. It's not that They don't get along (or at least I've never experienced a sense of Them disliking each other); They just don't work together, and perhaps often can't work together, because Their methods are antithetical to one another.

Nevertheless, if Hippolytos taught us anything, it's that mortals must never actively exclude any of the Gods from their lives. But then why and how would a follower of Artemis approach Dionysos? Or a follower of Dionysos approach Artemis?

I've pondered this a long time without really getting anywhere, and *Written in Wine* showed me why. Just about anything someone would go to Artemis for, they could also go to Dionysos for. It can't be an issue of *what* you ask each of Them for help with, but rather of *why* you ask for Their assistance.

It was the cult of Artemis and Dionysos near Patrai that actually helped me figure it out. That is the only place I know of where Artemis and Dionysos were actually worshiped together in the same festival, although even then they would have an activity for one, an intermittent activity, and then an activity for the other. The story goes (according to Pausanias' *Description of Greece* 7.19.1) that a priestess of Artemis Triklaria had a lover, but neither her parents nor his would let them marry, so out of desperation she had sex with him secretly in Artemis' sanctuary. Plague followed, and the oracle at Delphi revealed the lovers as the cause, and that Artemis required not only that the couple be sacrificed, but that every year the handsomest young man and most beautiful young woman would be sacrificed to Her as well (i.e., She was pissed). This practice was finally put to an end by Dionysos. A man came along with an image of Dionysos Melikhios that caused madness when it was looked upon. A festival replaced the human sacrifices, in which children wearing garlands of 'corn ears' would process down to the river Melikhios, dedicate their garlands before an image of Artemis, bathe in the river, put on new garlands made of ivy, then go to the sanctuary of Dionysos the Dictator, built for the image that was brought to Patrai. Burkert asserts that this festival would have included a maddened revelry of some kind, and while I have been unable to find direct evidence for that, the idea is not without reason: nine men and nine women would accompany the image to the river Melikhios, and this same image would inflict madness upon all who looked at it.

All this made me wonder: what was it about that madness – or at the very least a festival of the God of Madness – that made it the solution to the problems at Patrai? What if the act of a priestess of Artemis sleeping with her lover in Artemis' sanctuary was so incredibly polluted, so heretical that it could only be explained as madness? And what if, then, the only solution, the only way to end the punishment (meaning, at that point, the human sacrifices) was to sanctify that madness? And who better to sanctify madness than Dionysos? Human sacrifice would have been thought a type of madness by the ancient Greeks, but in the circumstances at Patrai it was a sort of necessary madness: an act of heretical madness had to be punished by a method of equally mad severity. This cycle of madness could not be wholly eliminated, but it could be brought into an acceptable and controllable structure: a festival of Dionysos. The cycle is broken and life is once again under control.

If all this is true, then when Artemis and Dionysos finally came together, it was when one thing needed to be destroyed and then replaced with another. This is, I think, the unique circumstance in which Artemis and Dionysos can work together. Sometimes one boundary isn't right and it needs to be torn down and replaced with another one. In this case one would need Artemis and Dionysos together, Dionysos to tear down the old boundary and Artemis to put up the new one. Neither of Them can do the whole job as effectively alone.

So, when might a follower of Artemis approach Dionysos? When some boundary or bond absolutely must be destroyed, when simply knowing and traveling through it isn't good enough and it must be taken down (and perhaps replaced by a new boundary by Artemis, or perhaps not).

And when might a follower of Dionysos approach Artemis? When there is a need for a boundary, or when a boundary can't be removed and must instead be fully understood and made permeable.

I think it might be hard for a follower of Dionysos to accept that sometimes boundaries really do need to exist, and I know it's hard for a follower of Artemis to let go of control even for a second. But every now and then it needs to happen.

Hymn to Artemis

by Rev. Lady Bella Sundancer

Hail Artemis, Lady of the Hunt
Lady of the Wild, Lady of the Free Spirit
Your arrows fly true, deadly and keen
But uncommonly gentle
Virgin pure, you bare yourself for no man
Running with your nymphs in an endless hunt
You heart is wildest ever, none could ever catch it
Though it is there for all to see
Lady of leaps and bounds, you soar
Beneath the silver crescent moon
The stars reflected in your eyes
All animals are your friends and hunt-mates
From the largest bear to the tiniest flea
There is nothing you haven't stalked
Nothing you haven't tracked and chased
Your eye is ever seeing, seeking new prey
Your bow is ready to draw, arrows set to fly
Lady of the Chase, you run for the freedom
For the gloriousness of the wild nature
None shall capture you, none shall corner you
You are fleet and graceful, adept and true
Mistress of the Wild, we pray to you
For your protection and for strength and surety

Invocation to Artemis

by E. A. Kaufman

Artemis of the Moon, Blessed Crescent, Bluest Sky,
Maiden of the Ways, Huntress.
Ariste, Calliste, Dafnia, Cynthia
Kourotrophos, Caryotis,
Hear this Daughter of the Moon,
Servant of the Gods, Priestess of the Old Ways.
You who protect the animals, I pay homage.
You who protect the wild places, I offer honor & praise.
You who are the Protectress of Women, I bow down before You.
All honor to You, Moon Bright.
All honor to You, Strong One.
All honor to You, Great Protectress.
Artemis of the Ways, Artemis who lights the Night,
Come, hear me, know my name, be with me.

Artemis

by Corbin

Long, long we wandered in your fertile wood,
Over stony banks and streams thick with rain,
Heard scatterings of rabbit and raccoon,
Listened for the secrets of the raven
Awaited the rising of the blistered moon.

Your silver shield, it beaconed like an eye
Through the clutching branches of the world
But where does it lead, O indifferent Huntress –
You who are so strong and chaste in youth,
Immortal, changeless, careless and aloof?

Will you bring us to a grove where Dryads dance,
Sweet wine is drunk and all Mysteries dispensed?
Or does some eerie cave await, a priest
With lonely brazier and pitiless knife
To cut away our robes, hopes, delusions,
To leave us naked in the night to face –
What?
The Minotaur of Crete, our inner beast?
A youth with shining brow and noble lyre?
Or merely an old woman, frail and wise,
Spinning a silvery wheel by a fire?

Hymn to Artemis

by Paul Derrick

Sacred virgin,
Lady of the Hunt,
Mistress of the Moon,
Artemis –
Hear me now as I sing of you.

I sing of your endless beauty,
Of your unswerving grace.
Of your weapons so fine,
And your impeccable eye.

I sing of your independence,
Of your incorruptible chastity.
Your unmistakable purity,
And your fierce protection of women.

Your mysticism also goes not unnoticed
You can conceal yourself from all eyes
With but a turn of the head and swish of the cloak
Stealth befitting of the Divine Hunter.

You who delight in the chase and kill
Yet also in song and dance and celebration
Who bestows strength and courage to those
Who have none –

Accept my song, for incomparable though it may be
To those of Olympos,
I pray it is worthy of you,
And that you may derive some small pleasure from it.

Memoirs of a Huntress

by Kayleigh Ayn Bohémier

I.

Some say that in the crying depths of the forest, trees moan like the hull of a ship, and that these soft-barked trees were made from a leviathan's bones. Artemis, that great huntress and wild Goddess, lashed ropes around the beast and drove it through Poseidon's waters until it heaved up on the land, dying instantly. She gave it to the land's people and distributed the meat among them, and then Artemis metamorphosed its bones. This is why the bark here is rough as decaying ivory.

II.

In the woods on top of a great boulder, Artemis sat repairing her carved bow while her hunting companions rested. A young woman soon stumbled upon the clearing and hailed the Goddess, but remained in the boundary between light and shadow.

"What do you want with the daughter of Leto?" one companion asked.

The woman said, "I would like to ask her what happened to the daughter of Agamemnon. I heard that Iphigenia was sacrificed to make favorable winds, or that Artemis took her to become a priestess, or that Achilles rescued her; what does the wild huntress have to say?"

Artemis laid aside her bow and sped to the ground as fast as a thought, slipping past her companions to where the woman stood. "Iphigenia was sacrificed for his transgression. Agamemnon would not escort his daughter to another home and no one would present her to another household shrine. Rather,

Iphigenia spent her life as my priestess; no mortal man could touch her."

III.

Imagine a beautiful woman with the libation bowl in her hands, one who pours out fresh milk in honor of Artemis. This priestess of Artemis stands bereft of mortal company. The hero Achilles stands beside her. Both of them stand frozen in time, these images on an amphora, as fire dances. A man's shadow casts the vase in darkness before he raises it in his strong arms. The small hands that close around his arms are ripped away. He dashes the bowl against the floor. Until his sandal strikes the fragments, the priestess's face remains intact.

IV.

No one remembers the bones. Few mention Iphigenia, priestess of Artemis. In the quiet forests, the Goddess's unaided hands hold the bow that strikes down animals and men alike. She deafens her ears to the new melodies that rise up to the heavens, creations that do not delight the Gods. The noise has spread across the globe.

Over the noise, Artemis smells far-off incense burned in her honor and hears voices stumbling through hymns in Ancient Greek. She puts her supple weapons away and walks across the mountains until she finds young men and women who honor her. Separated by distance, they do not know one another. She appears to one youth as a dark-haired maiden in a daisy-patterned dress.

"You burn those as though you have done it before," she says to him.

He blushes. "Truly, I have not – but one must always find amusements to pass the time." Brushing dark hair away from his face, he pokes the offering with a stick. "The old Gods are potent symbols. I like the idea of worshiping them."

"You would worship those you know almost nothing about?"

The man bites his lip and watches the smoke for a moment. "It is true that not much of the ancient ways have survived. I want to know more about them."

Artemis reaches for his hand, and as she does, gray fur spreads from his fingertips and up his arms. "Then come with me."

V.

Someone unearthed a statue of Artemis today. Its hands once held a bow and its nose is chipped. Through reconstruction, archaeologists can see what it once looked like: beautiful, painted, godlike. The devotees of this Goddess must have loved her.

Artemis watches them as they discover the secrets of her old temples. In those far-off places, the incense burns more regularly. She has come to know new lands and faces. The worship delights her, and it pleases her brother Apollon, who stands beside her. Laughing, they lock arms and look down on the patient supplicants.

Dianae Celticae

by P. Sufenas Virius Lupus

1. Abnoba

Hail to the goddess Diana
the undefeated huntress
in the northern forests

who between rivers
and on mountainsides
dwells in unspoiled splendor;

the Celts of Germania
know your name
and give you praises

as with loyal hound
and the songs of birds
you hunt down hares

and slay with your arrows
the mightiest of stags
in the dark woods.

Hers is the portion
best from every animal
slain in such sport,

her favors to those alone
who respect her domain
and do not encroach uninvited;

virgin indomitable,
slayer of beasts and men,

Abnoba the terrible–
with Diana your sister
guide my aim
and slay my quarry!

2. *Arduinna*

Praises to great Diana
the undisputed sovereign
whose groves are holy,

the refuge of slaves
and friend of foresters
across the western lands;

the Gaulish people
have called upon you
for health and succor

as you ride–
unprecedented the feat–
the fierce forest's boars

as if they were
the most docile of colts,
never to be broken.

She gives the gifts
of the boar in battle
to worthy heroes,

the ally of men
who gives unbidden
and takes undaunted;

virgin unquenchable
in the fires of ardor,
Arduinna most formidable–

with Diana your lover
stir my passions
for fair use of force!

3. Artio

I give glory to Diana
nurturer of children
in Alpine regions

as equally as you are
in far-off Athens,
Eleusis and Ephesus of envy;

the Helvetii tribe
honor your form
because of your blessings,

like the bowl of fruit
presented to bears
without fear of injury,

seated in majesty
with peace and contentment,
prosperity and nurturance.

To her the protection
of children is entrusted,
their safe births ensured,

their education enshrined,
and to mothers the aid
for relief of pain;

virgin unfathomable
in compassionate care,
Artio the amiable–

with Diana your mother
bestow the peace
of your safeguarded sleep!

Three Arrows

by Jennifer Lawrence

Laina shoved open the screen door and raced across the porch, taking the rickety wooden stairs two at a time. The spot under her left eye throbbed where the ashtray had struck it, and she could feel blood seeping from her nose. Her ribs ached where the nearly-full shampoo bottle had bounced off them, but that would fade quickly enough. She'd been hit often enough to tell which pains were just from bruises, when bones were broken...and when wounds would leave scars.

"Get back here, you *bitch!*"

She ignored Tom's voice and the rain pelting down from the midnight sky. The front door banged open behind her and she put on a burst of speed, bare feet slewing momentarily in the churned-up sea of mud that the front yard always became during a Wisconsin downpour. *Can't go back. Won't go back. I should have left the first time he hit me, but now ... with a baby on the way ... no. Never again.*

She had been able to hide the morning sickness from him for awhile – *morning sickness, hah! Morning, noon, and night, more like, or I wouldn't be spewing my guts into the porcelain altar at ten p.m.* – but he had come home tonight only an hour after he had left for the midnight shift at the cardboard box plant in Green Bay, before it had even started. He was ranting before he even got in the front door, snarling about being fired because he'd come to work drunk, and she could feel the cold dread settle over her like a wet blanket in February. Before she could rise from where she knelt on the bathroom floor, hunched over the toilet, he slammed the door open, calling her name.

It's his fault. He says he doesn't want kids, but he won't wear condoms, and he drinks up all the money so fast that when I run out of birth control pills, I don't have the cash to get the prescription refilled. The thought was as bitter as crabapples. The look in his eyes as he froze in the doorway, the stench of vomit floating thickly on the air, his already-angry features slowly mutating into the snarl of a rabid wolf, stuck with her as she reached the edge of the woods. Her heart rabbited in her chest as she ducked under the low-hanging branches of one of the junipers and paused to look back. He had disappeared from the front doorway, and for a moment, she dared to hope that the beer had gotten the better of him and he had gone to pass out on the sagging, cigarette-burned couch in the living room. The sweet, pungent scent of the evergreen tree surrounded her, one calming note in the symphony of terror that encompassed the last fifteen minutes.

But then his silhouette filled the door again, and she recognized the shape in his hands with a wrenching jolt of adrenaline that made her stomach knot in nauseous terror again. One of the reasons Tom had insisted on moving out of the city was so that he could go deer hunting again every fall, like he had with his father when he was younger. The shotgun he held carefully as he started down the stairs was an old one, gotten from a pawn shop in nearby Appleton, but it still worked just fine; he had brought down his limit of bucks each of the three years since moving out of Green Bay.

The thought of ending like those deer, splayed out and bloody on the leaf mold of the forest floor, was enough to break the paralysis that had claimed her. She whirled and dove deeper into the trees as he crossed the yard toward where she had disappeared, the rainwater plastering his straggling hair to his skull. "***Lainaaaaa!***" The roar echoed off the trees and was swallowed up by the darkness. "You've ruined my life long enough, you whore! If you think I'm going to clean out toilets in roadside rest stops to put food in the mouth of some other man's brat, you're wrong."

At least he didn't add, "Dead wrong," she thought wildly as she ran. Running for my life is so much better when I don't have to put up with clichés from bad 80s action movies at the same time. The cold was numbing her feet, and she was glad of it; he had started throwing things before she could get past him, blocking the way out of the bathroom. She could still smell cigarette ashes in her hair, down her shirt, and the hot, growing lump on her cheek suggested to her that the ashtray he had thrown might have broken the bone. When he had run out of things to hurl at her, she had uncurled from a ball, stuffed into the furthest corner of the bathroom, and run, shoving past him – a trick that never would have worked if he hadn't already been drunk and unsteady on his feet. But he was fast, even when plastered, and spun to grab at her long dark hair streaming out behind her as she rushed for the front door. Her scalp burned where he had torn out a handful of silky strands, and she'd had no chance to grab her shoes, coat, the car keys he'd thrown on the table, or anything else that might have helped. Broken twigs underfoot stabbed at the soles of her feet, and she winced at every flare of pain in instep and ankle.

Please please please let me get out of this alive, and my baby, too. She hadn't prayed since she was a small child, but the words unreeled themselves in her mind now without conscious will. *I know I was a stupid idiot to stay after the first time he hit me, but I thought I could change him. Should've known better. Love **doesn't** conquer all.*

The roar of the shotgun discharging was enough to leave her deaf, and Laina felt tiny metal pellets bite into her left hip, like being stung by a swarm of bees. Wet warmth trickled down her leg and she glanced down, dazed. The worn, faded denim of her jeans was growing dark, but in the shadows under the trees – dispelled only a little by the silvery radiance of the thin crescent moon above – she could see less than half a dozen holes in the fabric, spread out wide.

She resisted the insane urge to yell, "You missed!" at him and ducked past a thick-boled oak. That she was not dead from the shot meant that he'd gotten only a glimpse of her, or had slipped as he fired. The trees here were dense and their boughs had taken most of the damage. She pushed her way through a stand of wild raspberry bushes, the berries long gone – it was November, after all – and winced as the thorns raked her bare arms. The rain pouring down obscured other sounds – a double-edged sword, at best. *He can't hear it when I step on sticks and break them, and hiss when it hurts...but I can't hear him coming, either. Except when he yells. Or shoots at me.*

The leaves had almost finished changing colors with the cooler temperatures at night, she saw as she started up the hill. Wet, fallen leaves covered up the scree just under the topsoil, the result of years of erosion of the hills and cliffs in this part of the state. A layer of decaying foliage from the oaks and elms and maples, the color of butter and rust and blood, made the ground slippery. She felt her feet slide, grabbed a thin sapling, and dug the fingers of her other hand into the ground, pulling herself up little by little. She was wet to the bone, shivering uncontrollably, and knew that hypothermia was as apt to kill her as Tom's shotgun, if she couldn't get out of the cold and rain. Somewhere, very far away, she thought she could hear the high, belling howls of a pack of hunting hounds, and veered in that direction. *Another person. Safety. He wouldn't shoot me in front of a witness, would he?* She knew that finding someone else out here in the darkness – or a house – was her best hope. The highway was three miles away, back the way she had come, and their nearest neighbor's house was further than that. Her breath burned in her lungs as she ran, even as a frown furrowed her brow. *Someone out, this late at night, hunting? But it's still two weeks before Thanksgiving. Turkey season, yeah, but no one hunts turkey at night. Tom said deer season didn't start until the 22nd of November this year...at least, not for guns. It **is** bow season...but it's hard enough to hunt in the forest with a bow. Too great a chance an arrow would hit a tree branch instead of the target. Who'd make it worse by hunting in the dark? Aside from Tom, of course.*

She reached the top of the hill and crouched next to an old, mostly-rotten pine tree, whose lower branches had been broken off and whose bark was scraped back and forth with deep parallel gouges that exposed the white wood underneath. Dimly, her mind registered the markings, and she glanced up higher to see an opening in the trunk. A thin, sweet smell came to her – honey and beeswax mingled with the tree's pungent resin – and she lurched back up to her feet, pulling away, following the ridgetop. *Honey tree, and a bear's been visiting. Bad place to rest. A bear wouldn't kill me in a drunken rage, but I'd be just as dead. Though hopefully any bear in this forest is holed up somewhere warm and dry tonight. If he's smart.*

She hadn't heard Tom yelling for at least the last five minutes, and no further volleys of buckshot had come out of the darkness. Her hip had set up a low, steady burn, punctuated with the occasional flare of white-hot agony when she put too much weight on it. Worse than that, she could feel herself getting weaker, as the chill and the slow but continuous blood loss sapped her energy.

Lightning cracked directly overhead, arcing North to South across the sky in a silvery-blue spear of fire that made her flinch. The boom of thunder that followed almost instantly afterward was loud enough to drown out the persistent thrum of the falling rain. Laina blinked, trying to clear the dancing spots from her retinas. The lightning had cast everything into stark black-and-white relief, creating phantom shapes from conglomerates of branch and trunk and stone. *That cluster of boulders over there at the edge of the ridge looked like a pack of wolves,* she thought, starting forward again, *and I could have sworn that tangle of briar and hawthorn looked like a stag. Hell, the wind's blowing so hard, I could've sworn the waving branches were the buck tossing his head and shaking his antlers.*

"Laiiiiiinaaaa!"

She almost – *almost* – screamed. Tom's voice was close, too close, and for a moment, she couldn't feel her heart beating. With a low whimper, she scrambled forward through the underbrush, along one of the old deer trails, terrified back into incoherent prayer. *Please. Don't let him kill us. I can't make him believe this is his baby,* but I don't think he cares any more. We've never done anything to deserve this, never done anything to deserve him moving me away from my family, keeping me from my friends, burying me out here in the country in this ramshackle old farmhouse twenty miles away from the nearest town, cutting off the phone. And even if I had done something, the baby is innocent. Innocent. Please, please, is anyone listening? God, the devil...*someone!* I don't care who any more. It could be little green men from the Moon that comes to save me, and I wouldn't care. Please...somebody...

She stumbled forward through the woods, head bent as low as she dared, eyes fixed on the ground. The hills up here near the edge of the High Cliff State Park ran to steep bluffs with crumbling edges, and there were articles in the local papers on a semi-regular basis about campers and hikers who hadn't watched where they were going and stepped too near to the edge – or off it entirely. Nature could be unforgiving to the stupid and the careless.

"Stop right there, slut."

She froze. The words had been growled from right behind her, and a second later, the cold, wet metal of the shotgun barrel poked into the back of her neck. *Caught.* She Dimly, she felt her bladder let go, and he nudged her with the gun again. "Turn around."

She knew better than to think that she had any chance of fighting back – *what, his gun against...me throwing gravel and dirt at him?* – and did as she was told, a cold numbness spreading outward from the center of her chest. He stood there, as drenched as she was, even through the heavy camo jacket he had put on. There was a flat, satisfied smile stretching his thin lips, the smile of a lizard that has finally cornered the mouse it wants for dinner. Another flash of lightning lit up the scene: him, her, the crumbling rocks under her feet at the edge of the cliff, the thick cable of poison ivy stitched into the bark of the elm tree to her right, the dark, shaggy, shattered stump that loomed up behind

Tom, its two truncated forward branches looking for all the world like the outspread paws of a bear –

He spun around as the rain stopped, the wind shifting the clouds apart just enough for the argent light of the slivered moon to flood through, and for a moment, she thought the stump *was* a bear, jagged ends of the broken branches looking very like claws, the gnarl of woodscar growing over another terminated limb lower down the mirror image of an out-thrust muzzle. He flinched as the lightning flared again and the wind stirred the remaining leaf cover around them, the wavering leaves glistening in the rain and wind. Tom leveled the shotgun at the stump, eyes wide and wild, his reactions muddled with booze, and fired.

The sound was closer than it had been when he'd shot her, and for a moment, the whole world went silent. The moonlight brightened as the wind pushed aside further clouds, and before Tom could break open the gun at its breach and reload, he staggered. Laina flinched back as he half-turned; there was something long and bright projecting from his breastbone, and as she watched, another slender shaft sprouted from his groin. He dropped the empty Mossberg, hands going to his crotch, blood staining the faded fabric of his jeans. Even as his hands cupped gingerly around it, another streak of light icily swept past overhead and buried itself between his eyes.

He blinked, a thin rill of blood bubbling up from the arrow's shaft, and stared at her, dumbfounded. Then he fell forward like a rotten tree, landing face-down, driving all three arrows deeper into his body.

The rain stopped. Laina stared, unmoving, mouth open, not comprehending. He did not move, and after a long moment, she crawled forward on hands and knees to touch one of the bloodied shafts in wonderment. It was pale wood rather than fiberglass or aluminum, and the three-bladed, razor-edged broadhead shone bright as her mother's old earrings rather than with the dull blue-gray gleam of steel.

Light spilled down from the night sky, pouring into the clearing, and for a moment, Laina saw. The woman stood to the side of the bear-shaped stump, one breast bare, feet in sandals, wearing only a loose tunic of some old, foreign design. Her pallid hair was tied up neatly – much easier to travel through the forest without it getting tangled in thorns and weeds that way – and a pack of dogs cavorted around her feet. In her hands she held a silver bow, its graceful curve unfreighted by an arrow's weight now that her last shot was spent.

The woman smiled. It was a dangerous smile, wild and uncontrolled, but Laina's fear had evaporated, and tentatively, she smiled back. With a low, soft chuckle, the woman nodded, and then she was gone.

Laina blinked. The weather was clearing, and there was no fog to hide the woman, no sudden wave of clouds over the face of the moon to hide its light and allow the woman to slip behind the nearest tree. She had simply vanished.

She sat there in silence for a moment, tired, cold, wet, and hurting. *I could be mistaken, but I think the storm front has passed through. It even feels like it's starting to get a little warmer out.* She got stiffly to her feet, favoring her wounded hip. It didn't feel like any of the pellets had penetrated deeply enough to hurt the baby. Her fingers were almost numb with cold as she patted Tom's pockets and found his cell phone. Amazingly, she was high up enough on the ridge to get a clear signal.

"Thank you," she breathed. "For me and the baby, whoever you are."

Then, with shaking fingers but a slowly-calming heart, she dialed 911.

Artemis Hêmerêsia

by Frater Eleuthereus

I am the Soother of Arcadia.
Feel the comfort of the Moon, Sister
Though I am cloaked in the Night
I can and shall take the time
To hold you, suckle you, ease your pain

Come to me my lady and hero
As you clench in the pangs of birth
And sweat beads from you
I shall be there helping you breathe,
So that a little one can come forth bursting with life

Sometimes, though
Things happen that are so terrifying and cataclysmic
That your mind cannot comprehend
What your body has just endured
And you are at risk of shutting down

I am there too…
Listening, Silent, Comforting
I wish the aches could stop in a moment
But they won't
For you are but human, and even we Gods have limits

Not all battles are won with the force of fist, a blade or an arrow shaft –
Sometimes conflicts are won with patience, silence, and focus
By being the one who is just there
And doesn't leave when the crying begins and doesn't end
I would have hoped that men would have learned this by now

But in the millennia of time that I have circled the Earth and Sun

It has not come to pass yet.
And so I tell you
As I gaze in your eyes

Soon the shock will fade, and feel you shall.

I take note without judgment to your struggle
You did what you could
And now you do what you can
To rebuild and thrive –
I know you and that your womb will create again.

Traumas steal pieces of the souls of humankind
Boys, girls, women, men, all are victims to these harms.
Does it really matter, if we call these pains
Rape, abuse, kidnapping, torture, trafficking,
Or even miscarriage?

There are a million words in the realm of Hermes
To encapsulate these wounds
I shall not repeat them all.
For to me they are all wicked or tearful.
I Am here and won't let you go.

Pursue your fortitude like the stag drinking of the meandering river.
All rivers cascade and none are straight
Know too, that I am still there, even at 4 in the morning
When the nightmares wake up you- be Silent
Let Me in so I might share this burden with you.

Allow Me to watch and guard you with My quiver and bow, My whip and sword.
I will help you grow and be empowered-to learn from your pains.
Why use such primitive armaments?
Why such a wild demeanor?
Because now is the time to reconnect and become even better than before.

Nature is what I Am
I build respect and character –
Look at yourself in My reflection
Through time I wax and wane
So too shall your heart and feelings ebb and flow

That is emotion, your courage, your Humanity returning
You have the right to be safe and free
Let me help you to reclaim
That which is yours.
So your Inner Hero may come out my Shining Star.

Prayer and Devotion to Artemis

by Bia' Aletheia

Ritual performed on Samhain to request guidance and protection through the New Year.

O Great Artemis, Sister to Apollo, Favored Virgin Daughter of Zeus. Aristo, Great Priestess & Protector of Wild Things & Forest Nymphs. Chito'ne, Lady Huntress, the Far Shooting One with thy Golden Bow & Arrow. My'sia, Sweet & Fair Dancing Princess, a Light Bringer & Nursemaid of Children. O'rthia, Moon Goddess, Queen of Beasts, She who runs with Wolves & Stags. Parthe'nia, Lady of the Lake, Guardian to the Marshes and Wetlands. Phoebe, Beautiful, Chaste Maiden to Whom I feel a Special Devotion For. Soteira, Grant Us Your Guidance & Saving Graces During This Magickal Rite.

Provide offerings and libations

As I give you this offering and libation I ask in return that you favor us with Your attributes of physical strength, good health & endurance. See us through those perils that we may face in the mundane world. Keep a watchful eye upon Your children as we embark upon the New Year. We are thankful for your blessings and gifts that you have bestowed upon us. We honor Your presence here tonight as You guide us on our way. O Great Warrior and Untamed Spirit, shine down upon us from Thy throne. Hail Artemis, Aristo, Chito'ne, My'sia, O'rthia, Parthe'nia, Phoebe & Soteira.

Closing comments

O Great Queen of the Beasts & Fair Dancing Moon Goddess, I humbly thank You for Your attendance during this Magickal

Rite. Sweet & Pure Huntress Artemis, I bid You farewell and merry met. Until we meet again O Great Priestess & Protector of All Things Wild. Hail! Farewell & Merry Part to Thee, Daughter of Zeus

Artemis

by Patrick Corrigan

Lady of the Moon
Bringer of Light
Grant your daughter clarity of mind and surety of foot
Guide her well upon her path
Lady of the Silver Bow
Protector of Women
Grant your daughter safety and wholeness of mind, body, and soul
Guard her well upon her path
Lady of the Wilds
Virgin Huntress
Grant your daughter freedom of spirit, strength of self, and joy of innocence
Inspire her well upon her path
Lady of the Bear
Maiden of Childbirth
Grant your daughter ease, effortlessness, and gentle harmony
Soothe her well upon her path
Artemis Lokhia
Beloved Goddess
Smile upon your daughter
Oversee her rite of passage
Welcome her into Motherhood
Watch over her always
Blessed Be.

Gavrel

by Rebecca Buchanan

Author's Note: Inspired by the true story of Irena Krzyżanowska Sendlerowa.

The walls were taller than two men, stacked and quickly mortared, strung with barbed wire. In a few places, spikes had been driven into the mortar before it hardened, angled to catch and tear anyone trying to climb in or out.

Deep breath.

Clean air. This morning, at least, the wind blew away from the city, carrying the smoke and the smell of the camps.

Her feet crunched on the cold mud. The first frost of the season had already come in the night. It clung still to the air, despite the rise of the sun. For now, her shoes and socks and a thick pair of tights kept her warm; in a few weeks, the cold would be so deep that it would rise up through her shoes, up her legs, into her belly.

She wondered for a moment if the plants would keep running through the winter, or if the gas would be diverted to the front. Or to Berlin. People were already beginning to hoard coal, dig out old stoves that hadn't been used in a generation.

She glanced up at the high wall, at the wire and spikes, and at the graying buildings beyond. Dark windows. At least, out here, there was coal to be had.

She shifted her hips as she walked. The bundle around her waist moved, a bit, settling into a slightly more comfortable position.

Around the round corner in the wall. Another deep breath. Don't trip. They knew her. They would let in her. Let her out. Just like before, and the time before that.

She forced a smile as the wall straightened and the guards came into view. Three of them, at least that she could see, rifles slung across their shoulders. There was probably a fourth sleeping in the truck to the left of the gate. The other three lazed about, smoking, occasionally stamping their feet. But they wore thick dark gray coats and lined helmets covered their heads and thick boots covered their feet. They were not cold.

The one who was usually there – small brown eyes, scar beside his right ear – straightened when he saw her approaching. "Ah, Frau Schwartz, *guten morgen*. They have you out early today."

She waved a hand in irritation. "Ach, the Council tells me to go here, to go there, I go where they tell me." She stopped, digging into her coat pocket. "It's the way they live, you know, that's why I'm out here." She pulled out her permit and handed it to him. He glanced at it idly, handed it back, nodding.

"It's true. Live like animals, they do." He turned to one of the other guards, jabbing a thumb at the sad, sagging buildings behind them. "You should see the filth."

Frau Schwartz nodded, too. "They live like that, what do they expect? Disease. We're not careful, they could spread it to us. And I ask you, who wants a Jewish disease, hunh? Bad enough having to live next to them – I don't want to share their germs."

The two guards snickered. The third glanced in her direction, pulling on his cigarette.

She stepped through the gate, passed the hulking Panzerjäger – oh, another guard, in the seat, feet dangling over the back treads. She hadn't seen him. Five, then?? She waved a hand over her shoulder, forcing a casual tone into her voice. "I'll be back."

"Hey, Frau Schwartz, try to not to catch any of their Jewish bugs, eh?"

"From your mouth to the Fuhrer's ear!" she called back, waving again, and they laughed.

She dropped her arm. Deep breath. Walk casual. She fought the urge to adjust the bundle again.

This close to the gate, there were few people. No one wanted to be caught looking at the guards the wrong way, or not at all, or wearing the wrong color hat, or a pair of shoes that were too nice for a Jew and that a guard decided to take for himself. It was quiet, too, despite the fact that the ghetto had been crammed full of Jews and gypsies from all over Łódź and the surrounding country; too many people in too small a space. She glanced around, and saw an old man warily eying her from a doorway; it had been a grocery once, but the windows were bare. In that window over there, a woman who had been young once, her hair pulled back into a fraying knot; there was anger in her eyes.

Turning down an alley, Frau Schwartz caught sight of a woman standing against the surrounding wall, shawl pulled tight around her shoulders. She was looking around, right, left, right. She stepped aside suddenly and Frau Schwartz saw the small hole. A little girl crawled through from outside, legs and feet bare beneath her coat, hair in tangled knots; then a little boy with a hat, pushing a sack in front of him; and a dog with big ears. The children could not have been more than four or five years of age. The bag was grabbed by the woman, her hands anxious. She peered inside, then hugged the boy. Potatoes, maybe, or bones with a bit of meat and the marrow left.

The woman's head whipped around suddenly and she spied Frau Schwartz. She pulled the boy to his feet and hustled the children away, hugging the bag close. The girl dug in her heels. Her eyes – far too large for her head and very dark – locked onto Frau Schwartz. The dog growled.

Frau Schwartz looked away.

Clearing her throat, she turned into the building on her right. Tall and narrow and sagging, just like all the other buildings. She heard doors close as she stepped into the entryway. Up three flights of stairs, huffing a bit under the extra weight she carried. Through those closed doors she could hear coughing and soft arguing and crying. Even, muffled, violins and pianos and flutes; those few the Germans had not confiscated or destroyed as the Jews were driven into the ghetto.

The third floor, five doors down on the left. A number (303) was still nailed to the door. The paint was peeling and there was a deep gauge in the frame at knee level.

She listened intently for a moment, able to make out only soft voices and the occasional whimper. Finally, she lifted her fist and knocked, three times. The voices stopped. She knocked three more times. Quiet steps across the creaking floor. A male voice, trying to sound strong. "Yes?"

"Frau Bernardine Schwartz, Central Welfare Council. We had a report of typhus." She knocked again, voice commanding. "Let me in."

The door opened a crack and stopped with the chain pulled taut. A man with hollow cheeks and red eyes and a neatly trimmed beard looked out at her.

"Well?" She tapped her foot impatiently, wondering how many ears were pressed to the doors up and down the hallway. "Let me in, already."

A quick, abbreviated nod of his head. The door closed, the chain lifted, and the door opened again, wide enough for her to step through.

The apartment was tiny, maybe eight meters square. Just large enough for a bed, a small table with two chairs, a small stove and a row of cabinets along one wall. It was also neat. Hospitable. Normal. There were purple flowers in a cracked vase on the table; probably the last of the season. A few small pots of herbs grew on the sill of the single window. The floor was swept, the bed made.

A woman sat on the edge of that bed, body rigid. Her eyes were rimmed red. Her hair was neatly pinned up, the holes in her clothing neatly sewn. She held an infant in her arms, just a month old. She stared at Frau Schwartz, arms tightening until the infant squirmed in protest.

The man shifted his feet. Frau Schwartz noticed that the holes in his clothes were neatly sewn, too, but his shoes were deeply cracked. They would not keep his feet warm.

"What is his name?" She nodded at the baby.

The mother's voice was soft. "Gavrel."

"Ah." Frau Schwartz smiled and nodded. "A good name." Silence descended again. A few faint notes of a violin floated through the walls. "Very well, then." She untied and unbuttoned her coat, lifted her shirt, and began unwinding the bundle around her waist. A bag of flour fell into her hands. She set it and the wide strip of cloth on the table. "Enough for perhaps two weeks, if you ration it. Don't share it with your neighbors. They will wonder where you got it." The man shifted, as if to protest. "And they will ask questions," she persisted. "I don't want questions. Neither do any of the other parents. As far as everyone you know is concerned, Gavrel fell victim to typhus – like so many other children."

She grabbed one of the chairs and pulled it over to sit in front of the mother. The man followed and stood beside her, a comforting hand on his wife's shoulder. Frau Schwartz smiled down at the infant, at his deep blue eyes. "Good morning, Gavrel," she cooed. The babe twisted in irritation and frowned. He made a low, unhappy sound.

"I'm sorry," the mother apologized. She lifted him higher, closer to her breasts. "He's been like this all week."

"Has he eaten?"

"Yes, a bit. I can't get him to take much ..."

Frau Schwartz' eyes darted over the woman's shrunken frame. "Well, it will have to do." She pulled a small bottle from her pocket and unscrewed the cap, revealing an eyedropper. She saw the man's hand tighten. "Laudanum." She held the eyedropper over Gavrel's lips; one, two, three, four. "Not a strong dosage. Just enough to make him sleep," she assured them. "There we are, tak." She screwed the cap back on and tucked the bottle back into her pocket. "It will only be a few moments."

The father finally spoke. "How ..." he cleared his throat "... how will you get him out of the city?"

"I have papers drawn up. Fake name, fake birth date, but close enough; he looks the right age. The papers will get him to friends in Poznan, a church-run orphanage."

"A *church*?" His voice crept up in alarm and Frau Schwartz hastily waved her hands, shushing him.

"It doesn't matter," the mother blurted. "As long as he lives, it doesn't matter."

"Yes, he will live." Frau Schwartz looked up at the father, chewing on his lip. "I can assure you, the sisters there will not be baptizing and converting your son. They are only interested in protecting him. I keep a list, secret. And I promise you – as I promised the other parents – when this war is over, I will bring your son back to you." There was wild and confused hope in their eyes, and she had to look away, down at Gavrel. "Ah." She nodded in satisfaction. "Sound asleep." She looked back up at them, but found that they were looking at Gavrel, too. "I must take him now, before he wakes up."

Standing, she slid her arms beneath the baby, between the baby and his mother's arms. The arms tightened for a brief moment, and then sagged open. Frau Schwartz set Gavrel on the wide strip of cloth on the table, wrapped it around him a few times, and then lifted the whole bundle and tied it around her waist. She tied it securely; not too tight, but enough to hold the child in place, leaving his mouth and nose uncovered. She pulled her shirt down and buttoned up her coat. Once again, an overweight, middle-aged bureaucrat.

"Look the same, tak? Yes?"

They nodded, mute. The mother was leaning slightly forward, fingers pressed over her mouth. She sprang to her feet suddenly and rushed two steps forward – and stopped, hesitating, then gently pressed her hand to Frau Schwartz' belly.

Frau Schwartz covered her cold hand with both of her own. "I may be German, but I am no Nazi. My family has lived in Łódź for four generations. I will protect your son."

And she turned on her heel and was out the door, stomping authoritatively down the hallway. She heard the door close behind her, and weeping, and violin music.

Down the stairs, down more stairs, back out onto the street. Up the alley – no sign of the woman and the little children and the dog – and down the main street, back to the gate. No old man, but, yes, the woman with angry eyes.

"Done already, Frau Schwartz?" the friendly guard called.

"Ja." She smiled. "One less Jew to worry about. And they cried like they actually mourned the little brat." She shrugged, handing over her permit again. The guard didn't even bother to look at it this time, just handing it right back. The guard sitting on the back of the Panzerjäger laughed loudly and banged his heels against the metal. She felt a squirm against her belly and kept the smile on her face. She tucked the permit back into her pocket. "No doubt I'll be back here again soon." She waved. "*Auf Wiedersehen.*"

Mud crunched and squished beneath her heels, beginning to soften under the midmorning sun. The bundle shifted against her belly again. She tried to walk normally. A soft mewl. The guards were still talking. A few more steps. A louder whimper. Again. They stopped talking.

The friendly guard. "Eh, Frau Schwartz ...."

A louder yowl.

"Frau ...."

Stop? Keep walking? Her heels stuck in the mud.

She half turned her head. Their guns were off their shoulders. The guard asleep in the truck was peering out the window.

"Frau! Warten! Halt! – aah!!"

She was running now, head still half turned. The dog with the big ears. His teeth were buried deep in the guard's calf, pulling him down to the ground. A second guard leapt to his comrade's defense, swinging his rifle around to shoot the hound. The dog jumped before he could fire and Frau Schwartz saw red around the dog's mouth and then more red bubbled up as his teeth closed around the man's throat.

The guard in the truck threw open the door and began to climb out. With a loud clang, a rock slammed into his helmet and he fell to the ground, groaning, clutching his head.

Frau Schwartz rounded the corner of the wall, one hand clamped protectively beneath Gavrel. She just caught sight of the little girl, just inside the gate. The girl smiled. A ferocious, fearless, feral smile. And then she turned and was running, running lightly across the cold, sucking mud and the remaining two guards took off after her. Frau Schwartz looked away as the wall rose up beside her, trying to concentrate as she slid and stumbled, praying that the child would escape her pursuers in the maze of the ghetto.

Panting, she turned another corner, and another. She couldn't go home. No, not home. She would have to go to Poznan. Gavrel whimpered and squirmed, twisting the cloth tighter. Frau Schwartz slid to a stop and ducked into a recessed doorway. She would have to go to Poznan. She pulled open her coat and lifted her shirt. Gavrel squalled as she pulled him free. She held him up and stuck her finger in his mouth, giving him something to suck on. He scowled at her.

Cautiously, lungs dragging, Frau Schwartz tipped her head out of the doorway. Left, right, left. No signs of pursuit. She tried to quiet her breathing. No shouting, either. Back into the doorway. "All right, little one, you have to be quiet now, tak?" She nodded encouragingly. "Yes, you do." Gavrel curled his lips in displeasure. "Right, let's go than."

She stepped out of the doorway. Down the alley, down another. Try to look normal. Gavrel mewled. Up another side street. It would take days to walk to Poznan. She couldn't risk the train. She would need milk for Gavrel. Maybe –

Frau Schwartz stumbled and tripped to a stop, shoes slick. She gasped. The little girl stood before her, legs bare and muddied, hair a tangle. The dog stood at her side, fully half the girl's size. "Child ... Child, the guards ... how ... where ... careful ..."

The girl's lips curled in distaste and disappointment. "They're gone. They're stupid. I don't like stupid." She walked towards Frau Schwartz, bare toes curling deep into the mud. The hound padded along beside her, tail wagging, ears perked.

A dirty hand touched little Gavrel's forehead and he stilled his whimpers, hiccupped once. He smiled. " ... Piano," she said. She looked up at Frau Schwartz, eyes too deep and dark. The girl–

child pressed a finger to Frau Schwartz' lips. "You're brave. I like brave."

And she turned away, skipping, running, one hand buried in the thick fur of the dog's back. She stopped just at the end of the alley, and turned and smiled again. "Make sure he learns piano. He'll teach geniuses."

And she skipped away, lost in sun and shadow, no footprints to mark her path. Only a dog's echoing howl.

Artemis-Nemesis/Diana-Adrasteia

by Frater Eleuthereus

I am the Amazon whose night blue eyes never close to the wonders or hurts of the world.
My eyes narrow and I see rape, abuse, torture, and trauma.
Pains that no Mother should ever have to see inflicted on Her sons and daughters
The aches of not only you, but multiple beings in myriad realities
By men without a care in their world but their egos and sick sport

But even one assault is the loss of an entire world.
Look carefully at where you were, and where you are going.
Will you have the courage to fight the vampires that invade your world?
Will you help a wounded one in need or walk by?
Will you brandish a sword or run like the others?
That is my Challenge.
That is your Choice.

I watched you choose liberty and mercy, and smiled secretly in pride.
Walk with me through the torch lit halls of yesterday's pains and grief
Do not look too long lest madness befall you.
But know too that those hurts were seen and felt.
And Balance will return.
I promise.

I know what had to be, and I am sorry.
To Fate, all things must come to pass.
Even those things that no one wants or deserves
For especially in those eras are there lessons to be cherished
But still, even such as I cry.
What Mother would not?

My tears go from clear to black, corroding all they touch.
In the dark of night, call to Me, and I will listen.
I will put on my helm and armor.
Avenge you My children, I shall.
When the wicked laugh and imagine they have seized victory.
Let them think again.

And so it is,
In the glint of an astral arrow or a thrashing whip
That the justice of a time forgotten returns
I will be there to show all in this callous world
That every victim mattered and matters to someone
I will heal the wounds of the world,

One survivor at a time

The Savage Breast: Artemis of Ephesus

by Tim Ward

The following is an excerpt from Savage Breast: One Man's Search for the Goddess *(O Books, 2006), by Tim Ward. Used with permission.*

"Men of Ephesus, doesn't all the world know that the city of Ephesus is the guardian of the temple of the great Artemis and of her image, which fell from heaven?" - *Acts of the Apostles* 19:35[1]

The silversmith Demetrius called an emergency meeting of his guild. He warned his colleagues that the two things they cherished most were under attack: their goddess, and the income they derived from selling silver statues of her to the pilgrims who thronged to her great temple in Ephesus.

"Men," Demetrius declared, "you know our livelihood depends on this trade. You can see and hear what this fellow Paul is doing. He says gods made by human hands are not gods at all. Not only here in Ephesus, but all over Asia he has managed to convince people that this is the case. Now there's a great danger that our trade will come into disrepute. More than that, there is also the danger that the temple of the great goddess Artemis will itself come to be despised and even She, Artemis – whom not only Asia but all the world reveres – will be stripped of her greatness and come to mean nothing."

When they heard this, the men began raging through the street, shouting "Great is Artemis of the Ephesians!" They found one of Paul's traveling companions and hauled him into the theater. The mob had grown huge and wild. People shouted accusations and chanted over a Jewish representative's attempts to speak to them. But then the city clerk arrived.

"Men of Ephesus," he chided, "doesn't all the world know that the city of Ephesus is the guardian of the temple of the great Artemis and of her image, which fell from heaven? Therefore, since these facts are undeniable, you ought to be quiet and not do anything rash." He added that if the silversmiths had a grievance against these men, they could take it to court, and reminded them that they were in danger of being charged with rioting, which would bring the wrath of Rome.[2] It was a masterful blend of appeasement, reason, and intimidation, and the Ephesians left the theater meekly.

But Demetrius was right. Within a few centuries Christian emperors would ban all pagan practices. The temple to Artemis, four times the size of the Parthenon and one of the seven wonders of the ancient world, would be sacked, obliterated, its marble quarried to build churches, its statues ground to powder for making plaster. In 1860 it took a team of archeologists nine years just to find the temple. Today, only a single pillar has been re-erected. It stands in a swamp, like a lonely marble redwood, with a bird's nest on its crown.

Walking the excavated streets of Ephesus, less than a mile from the temple grounds, it was easy to imagine what the city must have been like in the first century A.D. when it was then the Roman capital of Asia. These days, foreigners again pack the ancient city, just inland from the Anatolian coast. The entrances are lined with souvenir shops, Turkish money changers, kiosks selling t-shirts and erotic postcards and, after a gap of 1600 years, statuettes of Artemis – plastic now, instead of silver. At the time of Paul the city had broad boulevards, public baths, gymnasiums, fountains, mansions for rich merchants, a port, the famous library that rivaled Alexandria's, and the great theater that was once filled with a bloodthirsty mob. A footstep carved in stone next to a drawing of a penis points the way to a local whorehouse. With half a million inhabitants, Ephesus was the New York of the ancient world.

"Devoted to dancers... the whole city was full of pipers and effeminate rascals and noise," wrote the ancient tourist Philostratus.

Paul urged the Ephesian Christian converts to shun the city's licentious ways.

"Be like God in true righteousness and holiness," he wrote to them. "Among you there must not be even a hint of sexual immorality, or of any kind of impurity....Nor should there be obscenity, foolish talk or coarse joking....No immoral, impure or greedy person – such a man is an idolater – has any inheritance in the kingdom of Christ and of God."[3]

The goddess was not so harsh in judging humankind. I thought in particular of the goddess Isis' appearance to Lucius, a poor lascivious soul transformed into an donkey by witchcraft in Apuleius' tale *The Golden Ass*. The story was written in the 2nd Century A.D., contemporary with the cult of Artemis of Ephesus, who like Isis was seen as a manifestation of the universal Great Goddess. After suffering humiliation and brutality, fleeing from those who wish to kill him, poor Lucius sees the full moon above the ocean, and he brays to the goddess for help. She rises up to greet him from the waves:

> All the perfumes of Arabia floated into my nostrils as the Goddess deigned to address me:
>
> "You see me here, Lucius, in answer to your prayer. I am Nature, the Universal Mother, mistress of all the elements, primordial child of time, sovereign of all things spiritual, queen of the dead, queen also of the immortals, the single manifestation of all the gods and goddesses that are. My nod governs the shining heights of Heaven, the wholesome sea-breezes, the lamentable silences of the world below. Though I am worshiped in many aspects, known by countless names, and propitiated with all matter of different rites, yet the whole round earth venerates me....I have come in pity of your plight, I have

come to favor and aid you. Weep no more, lament no longer; the hour of deliverance, shone over by my watchful light, is at hand."[4]

His salvation is to simply eat the petals of a rose. Freed from his donkey body, the restored Lucius enters the goddess' priesthood in Corinth, where he spends the rest of his days "enjoying the ineffable pleasure of contemplating the goddess' statue."

Apulieus' contemporaries in Ephesus would have understood exactly what he was talking about, and certainly they would know poor Lucius was not the only man who had to make an ass of himself before turning to the goddess.

In the Ephesus museum an entire hall is devoted to three life-sized statues of Artemis recovered from her temple. I sat on the cool marble floor of this hall and gazed up at her, my best shot at that 'ineffable pleasure' Apulieus described. The room is dim. Soft lights play on the idols' curves. Her face is impassive, her posture rigid. Her skirts flow down, making a single column of her legs. In the crooks of her outstretched arms she cradles two lions, reminiscent of the twin leopards from the Çatalhöyük goddess' throne, sculpted some 6,000 years earlier. Her hands reach out to her adorers as if to fold them into her. On her chest, beneath a zodiac necklace, she has rows and rows of breasts. Twenty, thirty, it's hard to count them all. They hang from her like clusters of grapes. She takes my breath away. It strikes me suddenly as so wrongheaded, the claim of scholars that she is a goddess of fertility. This Artemis does not remind me of birth. She's a goddess of abundance, of breasts overflowing, enough for all humanity to suckle.

To see them clustered there between her arms intoxicates me. It is the thing we were born to ache for. If Jung is right and there are archetypes hardwired into the brain, then the breast must be the most important: to press against it, latch, suck and gulp is the most primal human instinct next to drawing our first breath. Artemis of Ephesus, she opens it up in me, and I feel the need like a pang. I remember that the Spartans used to put male babies on a mountain top for seven days after birth, then weaned survivors early. It made better soldiers, so they said. It gave them a kind of anger. If we are made to long for the breast, does *not* having it twist something in us, create an anger and a craving we must carry all of our lives? Especially men like me, born of a bottle-nursed generation, suckled with the taste of a rubber nipple. Is this the root of our culture's grand obsession with the real thing?

At age eleven I was flipping through catalogues in search of brassiere ads. I tore out pages of *Life Magazine* featuring topless Las Vegas showgirls or half-naked African tribeswomen and hid them in my closet. At thirteen, I was thumbing through *Playboy* magazines in the back of the local variety store, terrified I was going to be discovered in my depravity, touching only the edges of the pages so as not to leave a sweaty fingerprint – was somebody going to dust for fingerprints? I still remember the first time I softly placed my hand on the front of a girl's blouse. The ecstasy shivered in me that short instant until she gently returned my fingers to her shoulders. In a crowd, my eyes still find the woman in a low cut top. My head swivels on the beach. I feel the thrill to see the swell of them, the bounce of them, the gorgeous raspberry tips of them though a light summer dress. I think of pornography, strippers, advertising, the breasts pushed in our faces in the rush to get our cash. I remember sitting in strip bars, watching girl after girl expose her breasts for all to see, and me soaking it in like a drunk at his liquor, each pair revealed leaving me wanting to see the next pair and the next and the next, though almost all were pumped and artificially rounded, an identical army of Barbie dolls. In the raw magazines, women's breasts are distended until they are grotesque, and it seems there is no limit to the flesh men crave. Imagine if Artemis of Ephesus could be our centerfold, if multiple breast enhancements became the newest fashion, each woman sporting a dozen, twenty, thirty breasts. Would that assuage this need we have, for more, more, more?

Strange how all the breasts we see today never fill us up. They leave us wasted, yet still wanting. What happened that we turned them into a commodity, silicon pillows to be devoured with our eyes? In the act, we lost them, or they somehow eluded us, because what they provided was never in the breasts themselves. Artemis of Ephesus symbolizes a kind of giving we no longer understand. Not an exchange, not love returned for love or money, but a flooding forth from her abundance. This is the goddess that Lucius turned to, a goddess so full that our need, our "depraved and sinful nature," is not an obstacle to her blessing. She gives because she is that giving. And what was my life, but a longing for this abundance, coupled with the belief that it doesn't exist?

It makes me want to push those breasts away. At the feet of Artemis, I realized I am a member of the cult of scarcity, that tribe that believes there is never enough to go around: not enough food, not enough money, sex, or love. I grew up in a prosperous middle class family. I have a job, a child, a lover, a hundred times more security than any other human generation has ever known. And yet I fear that it will all be snatched away someday. So I better not to take too much, want too much. Luxury is abhorrent to me. I call it thrift, but it is fear. Sometimes I envy members of that other tribe, the cult of abundance for whom life is overflowing, and they can easily reach out and grab that teat, and suck, and trust that there will always be milk, and not a vulture's beak.

I asked Teresa once how North American women felt about their breasts. Her answer surprised me.

"Your breasts give you your identity," she explained. "You see it happen at puberty. Girls who develop big breasts get all the attention from boys. They don't have to be smart or even develop much personality. Girls with small breasts, they either develop their brains or character and carve out an identity, something distinctive as a way to be noticed or win power in the same arena as men. If they don't have that spark, they become wallflowers."

"What about you?"

"Oh, I developed early. In grade six, the boys would sing at me 'way down yonder in the land of cotton,' because they thought I stuffed my bra. But I was a real introvert. The attention from boys didn't really affect me one way or another, because I didn't need it. Of course, later on that meant I could easily get whatever attention I might for a moment want, and that was sometimes nice. But I think it was hard for girls who had big boobs and a strong personality. They wanted to be accepted for who they were instead of for their breasts, and that screwed them up worse than all the rest of us."

Artemis, if men had you to look on, would it bring relief to the female sex? Could we bring our ache and craving to you, gaze upon your breasts, and then perhaps look women in the eye?

The Ephesus guidebooks say that these days most archaeologists don't think the lumps on Artemis' chest are really breasts, but rather the severed testicles of sacrificial bulls – fertility offerings that were part of her sacred rites. Historically, severed testicles were intimately associated with both Artemis and Anatolian Cybele; her priests cut off their genitals to honor her, and only a man thus unmanned could preside over her temple rites. Some scholars believe these eunuch priests originally conned their way into an earlier hierarchy of priestesses, eventually gaining power and taking over. The robes of Christian priests and the vow of celibacy which they take may be relics of this revolution. Others interpret ritual emasculation as a rite of gender-change: men so drawn to the goddess that they rend themselves to attain her image. The Romans called these self-castrators *Galli*, and their cult flourished in the heart of Rome. During Cybele's festivals there, scores of men in frenzies of devotion would slice their manhood off, and throw the severed organs in a great bloody heap. This gruesome rite appears again and again in the Near Eastern myths of Attis, Adonis, Tammuz and Osiris, the severed penis a fertile agent of rebirth. In this way the priests of Artemis re-enacted, bloodily, the sacred sacrifice of the ancient kings, whose death brought new life to the land, and in this they earned their role as counterpart, and eunuch consort to the Goddess of all abundance. Which is it, breasts or testicles? An icon may have many meanings. At least one statue of Artemis of Ephesus has clearly defined nipples.[5] But now I see the goddess with a disturbing double vision: with both breasts and swinging testicles around her neck. The gift of abundance and the brutal price that gift demands.

To receive that breast, did one have to become her eunuch slave? I had to laugh. Too many of my past relationships had been with the likes of Artemis. Sooner or later, I would be cutting off my balls so she could sling them around her neck. I believed with each relationship that this act was necessary, and would lead to some epiphany. Instead I just lay there bleeding. Eventually I hardened my heart to Artemis' kind. Her offer of the breast took too much from me. I wonder if Paul hit a chord with the Ephesians of his day when he wrote to them, "Wives, submit to your husbands as to the Lord."[6] Once the woman submits, once she is property, then her husband owns those breasts, those clusters of abundance. No need to slice off your balls to get them. And yet it has not worked out well for men these past 2,000 years. Those breasts still hang before us, a promise and a torment, ours to possess in marriage or the marketplace, and yet strangely out of reach.

At times when Teresa lies naked within my grasp, I feel such hatred for her breast. I clutch it in my hand as if it were a dove about to take flight. I want to possess it and tear it at the same instant, want to make it mine and to hurt it. This breast, the thing I want so much, the thing I believe I will never have. And when I reach my frenzy, there are times when I'm suddenly the boy again, the boy at her breast, and I want it with a fierce craving, I clutch it and I am stricken with terror that it will go away. It's worse than the vulture's bite. I hate her then, I hate her most when I want her breast like this, hate the helplessness of the need, the helplessness I feel in her arms, because nothing matters like the nipple in my mouth, and I disappear into it and suck so hard I know it hurts her, hurts her with the pleasure of the sucking need in me. They make me savage, craven, dependent. And what bliss it is, locked in Teresa's arms, to feel that hate and let it pour out, while I lie pawing at her breast.

From the ruins of Ephesus, Teresa and I drove up the slope of Nightingale Mountain on the outskirts of the modern town, to a large gravel parking lot crammed with a dozen tour buses and perhaps a hundred cars. The crowd swarmed around us, tour group leaders shouted for order and waved their pennants as a steady throng pushed through the entrance and past the many kiosks of this most visited of all Ephesus' historical sites. On this hilltop, the statues and portraits that the venders sell are not of Artemis, but of the final form the goddess took at Ephesus: as Mary, Mother of Jesus.

According to early church tradition, several years after Jesus' crucifixion, his mother came to Ephesus with the disciple John. She lived here for many years and by some accounts, died and was buried on this hillside. A 19th century German nun, Catherine Emmerich, had a series of visions describing the exact location of the house where Mary lived, and wrote a book about it. In 1891, members of the Lazarist Order of Izmir followed the directions of those visions and uncovered a 6th century A.D. dwelling with foundations dating back to the time of Christ. Today the House of Mary is venerated as a Catholic shrine. Pope Paul VI and Pope John Paul II have both visited it. No gravesite has been found however, and there's no encouragement from the Church to look for it, as that would go against the Catholic doctrine of the Assumption, that Mary never died, but ascended directly to heaven.

Was it coincidence that Mary came to be identified with the city of the Great Goddess Artemis? As the Turkish director of the Ephesus museum subtly put it in the official site guidebook, "Since the Virgin Mary possessed many of the virtues of Artemis, the most magnificent goddess, the new religion [of Christianity] gained popularity in Ephesus."[7] In fact, the edicts of the Christian emperor Theodosius banned all pagan practices and closed all temples at the end of the 4th century A.D. Under threat of death and torture, those who worshiped Artemis of Ephesus could no longer practice openly. So they renamed her Mary, and simply carried on. Local goddesses all across Europe assumed new identities as Madonnas and blessed virgins under the intolerant new religion. But the first church in all of Christendom dedicated to the Virgin was established here in Ephesus.

Then in 431 A.D., a great church council was convened at this site to settle a controversy that was ripping the newly powerful religion apart: Was Mary the Mother of God, and thus quasi-divine being to be reverenced, or was she the merely mortal mother of a fully human Jesus, who only received the spirit of the Christ upon his baptism? Two hundred Church authorities debated the issue for three months, in the end declaring Mary both mother of the human Jesus and of the divine Christ. As a footnote, they declared officially that Mary was buried here (an assertion that is still the subject of dispute).

Teresa and I joined the crowd along the wooded path to Mary's house. We passed a fountain, flower gardens, and eventually arrived at the humble brickwork dwelling with a packed earth floor. Two Franciscan monks with tonsured heads and hooded brown robes (a costume similar to those first priests of the goddess) guarded the door, preventing entry without the proper dress. Inside, a simple black statue of the Virgin stood surrounded by fresh flowers, her arms outstretched to the believing masses. These people were not tourists like the ones at Ephesus. They were pilgrims, pressing towards the statue with prayers of supplication, praise and gratitude. They lit candles, put offerings in a box by the wall. Some wept, some gazed in silent rapture. What was the difference between this scene and the worship of Great Artemis that Saint Paul decried? Nothing but the size of her temple and the clothes she wore. And if one were to pull aside the Blessed Virgin's modest robes, how many rows of breasts might one find hidden underneath?

The loud praying and crying had a weird effect on me. Although I could contemplate Artemis in a museum with a sense of awe, I found the shrine of Mary stifling. I just wanted to get out, quick.

"Come on," I whispered to Teresa as we shuffled towards the statue, "they found a house through a sickly woman's dream? How hard could it be in Turkey to find crumbling bricks on a hillside? What does that prove? And look at all these people flocking here like sheep. At least the temple of Artemis was marked by her image which fell from heaven – a meteorite of some sort, an actual event. But this is just superstition."

Teresa, a Catholic, refused to argue. She lit two candles. One for her daughter, one for me. Her eyes questioned my scorn, and I had to laugh. The old Protestant in me has more trouble with Mary than with Artemis. Or was it that I was far more comfortable sitting at the feet of a dead goddess than a living one, one who might answer my prayers, and in return place her demands on me?

"Where's your flower?" Teresa said out loud in her sleep, tossing restlessly.

We were in Istanbul, still adjusting to the shock of a Muslim culture after so many days in ancient goddess temples.

Sometimes Teresa sleepwalks when she's stressed. Usually I catch her before she gets out of bed and can talk to her while she dreams. I tell her she doesn't have to go anywhere, and usually she will lie still again.

"What flower?" I replied.

"Everybody in the stadium's got a flower. Except you."

"Will this do?"

"Oh, yeah. But it's not good here. I wish you'd get out of here."

"What do you see?"

"The little stadium, full of men. They are all waiting for something. Chanting on their prayer beads. It's dusty. The land around is dry. They aren't happy. There's a meanness. They want something, that's why they came here. It's like a thirst in them, a craving. They think this meeting will give them what they want, but it won't. The meanness will just grow harder. They are watching you now out of the corner of their eyes. They know you're not one of them."

I had never heard her give such vivid descriptions while dreaming. I could picture an ancient amphitheater, like the one at Ephesus, as if I were inside the scene with her.

"Now a big man in long robes is entering the center of the stage. Everyone is watching him. He's got a long grey beard. Next to him is a pile of body parts. A woman's body parts. He's picking them up one by one, and he's naming each dismembered part as a part of the chant.

"Now the men at the bottom of the stadium are standing, lining up. The big man in robes, he's hitting them one by one with one of the body parts. Hitting them with it like a club across the face. Then each of them falls down in a trance. I'm scared, really, really scared that the big man is going to do this to you. The men at the top of the stadium are looking at you openly now. They are coming for you. Oh no! They are grabbing you, pulling you down to the front," her voice grew shrill and frantic. "The big man in the robes, now he's hitting you with the body part and everybody is chanting."

"What am I doing?"

"You're not in a trance, you're fighting it. But you can't last. Little by little you're falling under it. It's so horrible to watch."

Her breath came short and shallow, her body tensed. I thought I would have to wake her, but I hated to destroy the scene she had created, the purpose the dream carried.

"You have to help me," I said.

She twisted, eyes rolling behind her closed eyelids.

"Yes! Now I'm rushing into the stadium and, and I push the big man down. I grab you and pull you out of there. But you're pretty much gone. You stumble like a zombie as I drag you along. The men are chasing us. We run over the streets. They can hear our feet on the stones. They are going to get us. There's no escape in this city. I'm scared."

"You've got to find the place where we can be safe. Look for it."

"Here!"

"What do you see?"

"A circle carved in the stone floor. We're standing on it now. I put my hand on it, and it starts to glow. Now it's sinking. We're going down under the street. It's glowing under here, warm and glowing. I can hear the men running on the streets above, looking for you. You're safe now. But it's no use. There's just a tiny bit of you left. The trance has taken over, you're almost gone." She wailed thin and low.

"Sooner or later they will find you. I put you in my lap and take your head in my hands and wait. I put your lips to my breast and oh, like a baby you're drinking from me. Drink, my beautiful boy, drink....But I know you are going to go back to them. I know the trance will work on you too, because you want it to. Something in you wants it to. It won't do you any good, what they have, but there's a piece of you that is drawn to it. You'll go back, you'll go back. Oh, I want to take away that piece in you..."

"But it's my piece," I said softly. "You can't take it from me. You can't fix it for me. It wouldn't be right."

She cried in her sleep. Then suddenly: "Something's opening up in your chest, like a door to a room. I can go in through it. It's dark inside. Dank, hollow, vast. There's fear here, terror. Things are moving along the walls and corners inside of you. Dark, slithering things. They don't look at me. I can't see their eyes.

They are keeping their eyes averted from me. But this is what I love, these dark things. I love them. I want them. So beautiful.

"The terror in the room is going now. It's working. You're coming out of the trance. I'm walking out of your chest and you're okay now. You're safe. You're asking what happened, and I tell you, 'Nothing, nothing, we just stopped to rest.'"

"We get back in our dusty little car, and start to drive away..."

She fell silent. I woke her up gently before the dream could vanish and told her what I had heard. She remembered all of it, and filled in more details. The flower was like a blue lily. The city streets were like the ruins of Ephesus. When we came to the part about her desire for the dark slithering things in the room, it seemed so real that it became suddenly erotic. I slid on top of her, and the dark goddess came out in her immediately, as if she had been waiting. I knew that it was *she* who wanted to take those sickly pieces away, that behind the loving concern for me in her dream was Hekate's craving to eat those twisted parts of me.

I felt the hunger in her jaws. I looked into those ancient eyes, black and frenzied, teeth gnashing, bone fingers drawing me to her like dinner. A flood rolled through me like a wave, up from my feet though my legs, rising up to my belly and then pouring into her, pouring out through my body and my eyes, as if emptying out my essence. All that was left was a skin, a hollow thing hanging in space, clinging to her arms. I felt cold, paralyzed. How will I get back from inside of her? The thought was a thin flicker, a wisp in a void. I had no will.

I floated with no sense of time. Suddenly something welled up like a spring, trickled in, like filling up an empty flask. It didn't come back to me from her. Instead, it seemed I could grow this strange thing – a center, spirit, I don't know what to call it – inside of me again. It was like a snake growing a new skin, but on the inside, or a moon waxing full after its time of darkness. It could be born in me again. Yes, that was the myth: the god cut down to die and live again: horned god of the moon, bull-god of the sacrifice, the Eleusinian ear of grain, reaped.

"Did you feel it?" I asked her later when we could once more speak.

Teresa nodded. "Yes, it was like you poured into me. This is what I wanted since the first day I saw you. You fed me from the inside, the thing that I was so hungry for, that makes me so frantic. For the first time I feel full. It happened, it finally happened. You really did pour into me..."

She rested her head on my shoulder and breathed deep.

It hit me at that moment that I had misunderstood the meaning of Hekate's fierce hunger. Maybe it was not an urge to destroy, but to absorb the essence of men, while somehow leaving us intact. Perhaps by surrendering to Hekate's hunger, we men, just like the sacrificial year gods, can gain Artemis' abundance. I realized I was jumbling together myth, metaphysics, love and sex. Even so, my conception of the conflict between Artemis's abundant breasts and Hekate's consuming jaws had changed. I had thought of these goddesses as irreconcilable opposites, incarnate in every woman, like the light and dark phases of the moon that Artemis and Hekate embody. More truly like the moon, perhaps these goddesses are not opposites, just different faces of the same force.

Then I thought about the slithery parts of my own unconscious mind. In her dream, Teresa said that these were the things inside all men that made them fear and hate women, and that they fueled the angry male religion she had witnessed in the stadium. But what I did not see until this moment is how similar my slithery things are to Hekate's creatures: snakes, toads, spiders.... It struck me that these creatures are the projections of man's own darkest anima onto the witch. What are those slithery things? Why does Teresa love them even though they mean her harm? I reach in and stir the pot of my own unconscious. Dark, twisted fragments roil to the surface – rage, hatred, spite, loathing, domination, and fear. They speak a language of cruelty, violence and lust. The slime that covers them is guilt and shame. No wonder they seek to hide beneath the surface of my conscious mind. Yet I cannot turn my face away from women, for these slithering things, destructive as they are, draw me to the feminine more fiercely than my desire for a happy romance.

Suddenly I understood. Of course Teresa loves these things in me. They are the shadow forms of my own most desperate need of her. My love and my anger towards women are not two opposite, irreconcilable emotions, but two expressions of the same basic need: the rose and the thorn growing from the same stem.

I lay in bed, gazing out through the window at the moon over Istanbul. Now what? It's all very well to have a flash of insight in the middle of the night, but is this really going to help change my behavior, help keep me from destroying yet another relationship?

---

[1] *New International Version (NIV)*.
[2] Ibid. Acts of the Apostles 19:24-41.
[3] Ibid, Ephesians 5:3-5.
[4] Apuleius, *The Golden Ass*, tr. Robert Graves, p. 265.
[5] See Baring and Cashford, p. 329.
[6] Ephesians 4:22 (NIV).
[7] Selahattin Erdemigil, *Ephesus*, p. 21.

Worshiper

by Thista Minai

Somewhere hidden in swirls of wild windblown hair
is a mystery of identity unbound.
Show me where the boundaries lie,
draw them clear and stand astride.
Show me how to travel through by knowing either side.

Freedom is the song upon my lips when I follow Your pursuit,
feet beating a rhythmic hunt,
heart beating in wild agreement.
Mind seething and soul bleeding,
I'll fall and be remade by You.

Always wreathed in yellow flowers, pitcher in hand,
I live for You.
Love finds form in purity,
grows into devotion, blooms into a priestess.
All my breath, laughter, tears,
All of it for Artemis

Suggested Reading

Secondary Sources

Blundell, Sue. *Women in Ancient Greece*. 1995. Cambridge, Massachusetts: Harvard University Press, 2001.

Burkert, Walter. *Greek Religion*. Trans. John Raffan. 1985. Cambridge, Massachusetts: Harvard University Press, 2000.

Burkert, Walter. *Homo Necans: The Anthropology of Ancient Greek Sacrificial Ritual and Myth*. Trans. Peter Bing. Berkeley, Los Angeles, London: University of California Press, 1983.

Burkert, Walter. *Structure and History in Greek Mythology and Ritual*. 1979. Berkeley, Los Angeles, London: University of California Press, 1982.

Cartledge, Paul. *The Spartans: The World of the Warrior-Heroes of Ancient Greece*. Woodstock & New York: The Overlook Press, 2003.

Chrimes, K M T. *Ancient Sparta: A Re-Examination of the Evidence*. 1949. Manchester, Great Britain: Manchester University Press, 1999.

Clark, Gillian. *Women in Late Antiquity: Pagan and Christian Lifestyles*. 1993. Oxford: Oxford University Press, 1994.

Cole, Susan Guettel. *Landscapes, Gender, and Ritual Space: The Ancient Greek Experience*. Berkeley, Los Angeles, London: University of California Press, 2004.

Condos, Theony, ed. *Star Myths of the Greeks and Romans: A Sourcebook*. Grand Rapids, Michigan: Phanes Press, 1997.

Connelly, Joan Breton. *Portrait of a Priestess: Women and Ritual in Ancient Greece*. Princeton, New Jersey: Princeton University Press, 2007.

Deacy, Susan and Karen F Pierce, eds. *Rape in Antiquity: Sexual Violence in the Greek and Roman Worlds*. 1997. London: The Classical Press of Wales, 2002.

D'Este, Sortia. *Artemis: Virgin Goddess of the Sun & Moon*. London: Avalonia, 2005.

Downing, Christine. *The Goddess: Mythological Images of the Feminine*. 1981. New York: The Crossroad Publishing Company, 1989.

Farnell, Lewis R. *The Cults of the Greek States*. Vol. 2. Oxford: Clarendon Press, 1896.

Guthrie, W K C. *The Greeks And Their Gods*. 1950. Boston: Beacon Press, 1955.

Hope, Murray. *Practical Greek Magic: A Complete Manual of a Unique Magical System Based on the Classical Legends of Ancient Greece*. Wellingborough, Northamptonshire: The Aquarian Press, 1985.

Kerenyi, C. *The Gods of the Greeks*. 1951. London: Thames & Hudson, 2000.

Kramer, Ross Shepard, ed. *Women's Religions in the Greco-Roman World: A Sourcebook*. New York: Oxford University Press, 2004.

Larson, Jennifer. *Greek Nymphs: Myth, Cult, Lore*. New York: Oxford University Press, 2001.

Lefkowitz, Mary. *Greek Gods, Human Lives: What We Can Learn From Myths*. New Haven and London: Yale University Press, 2003.

Lefkowitz, Mary R. *Women in Greek Myth*. Baltimore, Maryland: The Johns Hopkins University Press, 1986.

Melas, Evi, ed. *Temples and Sanctuaries of Ancient Greece: A Companion Guide*. Trans. Maxwell Brownjohn. London: Thames and Hudson, 1973.

Minai, Thista. *Dancing in Moonlight: Understanding Artemis Through Celebration*. Hubbardston, Massachusetts: Asphodel Press, 2008.

Otto, Walter F. *The Homeric Gods: The Spiritual Significance of Greek Religion*. Trans. Moses Hadas. 1954. London: Thames and Hudson, 1979.

Parke, H W. *Festivals of the Athenians*. 1977. Ithaca, New York: Cornell University Press, 1986.

Pomeroy, Sarah B. *Goddesses, Whores, Wives, and Slaves: Women in Classical Antiquity*. 1975. New York: Schocken Books, 1995.

Pomeroy, Sarah B. *Spartan Women*. New York: Oxford University Press, 2002.

Rice, David G and John E Stambaugh, eds. *Sources for the Study of Greek Religion*. Number 14, Society of Biblical Literature: Sources for Biblical Study, ed. Burke O Long. Scholar Press, 1979.

Schwab, Gustav. *Gods and Heroes of Ancient Greece*. Trans. Olga Marx and Ernst Morwitz. 1946. New York: Random House, 2001.

Simon, Erica. *Festivals of Attica: An Archaeological Commentary*. Madison, Wisconsin: The University of Wisconsin Press, 1983.

Sissa, Giulia. *Greek Virginity*. Trans. Arthur Goldhammer. Cambridge, Massachusetts; London: Harvard University Press, 1990.

Spawforth, Tony. *The Complete Greek Temples*. London: Thames and Hudson, 2006.

Vernant, Jean-Pierre. *Mortals and Immortals: Collected Essays*. Ed. Froma I Zeitlin. 1991. Princeton, New Jersey: Princeton University Press, 1992.

Von Rudloff, Robert. *Hekate in Ancient Greek Religion*. Victoria, British Columbia: Horned Owl Publishing, 1999.

Primary Sources

Aeschylus:	*Agamemnon*
	Suppliant Women
Apollodoros:	*The Library of Greek Mythology*, also known as *Library and Epitome*
Aristophanes:	*Lysistrata*
Aristotle:	*Athenian Constitution*
Bacchylides:	*Odes*
Callimachus:	*Hymns*
Diodorus:	*Library*
Euripides:	*Hippolytos*
	Iphigenia in Aulis
	Iphigenia in Tauris
	The Suppliants
Herodotus:	*The Histories*
Hesiod:	*Theogony*
	Works and Days

Homer:	*Iliad*
	Odyssey
Pausanias:	*Description of Greece*
Pindar:	*Odes*
Pliny the Elder:	*The Natural History*
Plutarch:	*Aristeides*
	Themistocles
	Theseus
Pseudo-Hesiod:	*Homeric Hymns*
Xenophon:	*Agesilaus*
	Anabasis
	On Hunting

Internet Resources

Temple of Artemis Cataleos:
http://www.cataleos.org/
Neos Alexandria temple page for Artemis:
http://neosalexandria.org/artemis.htm
Neokoroi temple page for Artemis:
http://www.neokoroi.org/artemis.htm
Theoi.com entry on Artemis:
http://theoi.com/Olympios/Artemis.html
Artemis: Greek Goddess of the Hunt:
http://www.paleothea.com/SortaSingles/Artemis.html
Thiasos Artemis:
http://groups.yahoo.com/group/Thiasos_Artemis/
The study of Artemis:
http://groups.yahoo.com/group/thestudyofartemis/
Virgin Huntress:
http://groups.yahoo.com/group/virginhuntress/

About the Bibliotheca Alexandrina

Ptolemy Soter, the first Makedonian ruler of Egypt, established the library at Alexandria to collect all of the world's learning in a single place. His scholars compiled definitive editions of the Classics, translated important foreign texts into Greek, and made monumental strides in science, mathematics, philosophy and literature. By some accounts over a million scrolls were housed in the famed library, and though it has long since perished due to the ravages of war, fire, and human ignorance, the image of this great institution has remained as a powerful inspiration down through the centuries.

To help promote the revival of traditional polytheistic religions we have launched a series of books dedicated to the ancient gods of Greece and Egypt. The library will be a collaborative effort drawing on the combined resources of the different elements within the modern Hellenic and Kemetic communities, in the hope that we can come together to praise our gods and share our diverse understandings, experiences and approaches to the divine.

A list of our current and forthcoming titles can be found on the following page. For more information on the Bibliotheca, our submission requirements for upcoming devotionals, or to learn about our organization, please visit us at *www.neosalexandria.org*.

Sincerely,

The Editorial Board of the Library of Neos Alexandria

Current Titles from the Bibliotheca Alexandrina:

Written in Wine: A Devotional Anthology for Dionysos
Dancing God: Poetry of Myths and Magicks by Diotima
Gods and Mortals: New Stories of Hellenic Polytheism by
    H. Jeremiah Lewis
Goat Foot God by Diotima
Longing for Wisdom: The Message of the Maxims by Allyson Szabo
The Phillupic Hymns by P. Sufenas Virius Lupus
Unbound: A Devotional Anthology for Artemis

Forthcoming Titles from the Bibliotheca Alexandrina:

Words of Power: A Collection of Modern Greek- and Egyptian-Themed Fiction in Honor of Thoth
Waters of Life: A Devotional Anthology for Isis and Serapis
The Balance of the Two Lands: Writings on Greco-Egyptian Polytheism
    by H. Jeremiah Lewis
Echoes of Alexandria: Poems and Stories
    by H. Jeremiah Lewis

Printed in Great Britain
by Amazon